Five Risks Presbyterians
Must Take for Peace

Five Risks Presbyterians Must Take for Peace

Renewing the Commitment to Peacemaking in the PC(USA)

Christian Iosso

WESTMINSTER
JOHN KNOX PRESS
LOUISVILLE · KENTUCKY

First edition
Published by Westminster John Knox Press
Louisville, Kentucky

17 18 19 20 21 22 23 24 25 26—10 9 8 7 6 5 4 3 2 1

Book design by Sharon Adams
Cover design by Mary Ann Smith

Library of Congress Cataloging-in-Publication Data

Names: Iosso, Christian, author.
Title: Five risks Presbyterians must take for peace : renewing the commitment
  to peacemaking in the PC(USA) / Christian Iosso.
Description: Louisville, KY : Westminster John Knox Press, 2017. | Includes
  bibliographical references. |
Identifiers: LCCN 2017006622 (print) | LCCN 2017033296 (ebook) | ISBN
  9781611648232 (ebk.) | ISBN 9780664262853 (pbk. : alk. paper)
Subjects: LCSH: Reconciliation—Religious aspects—Presbyterian Church
  (U.S.A.) | Peace—Religious aspects—Presbyterian Church (U.S.A.) |
  War—Religious aspects—Presbyterian Church (U.S.A.) | Presbyterian Church
  (U.S.A.)—Doctrines. | Presbyterian Church—Doctrines.
Classification: LCC BX8969.5 (ebook) | LCC BX8969.5 .I57 2017 (print) | DDC
  261.8/732088285137—dc23
LC record available at https://lccn.loc.gov/2017006622

Most Westminster John Knox Press books are available at special quantity
discounts when purchased in bulk by corporations, organizations,
and special-interest groups. For more information, please e-mail
SpecialSales@wjkbooks.com.

To all the participants in the Peace Discernment Process from the congregations, presbyteries, and General Assembly Peacemaking Committees of 2010, 2012, 2014, and 2016;

to the Peace Discernment Steering Team: Shaheen Amjad-Ali, J. Mark Davidson (chair), Jessica Hawkinson, Craig Hunter, Kathryn Poethig, Shaya Gregory Poku, and Roger Powers;

and to stewards of Presbyterian Peacemaking from whom I have learned much: E. William Galvin Jr., Sara P. Lisherness, Edward L. Long Jr., Donald W. Shriver Jr., Ronald H. Stone, and the late Robert Smylie.

Contents

Text Boxes

Foreword

After sixteen years of war, overheated fears of terrorism, and the constant sound of gunshots on our streets, some may say that the churches have given up on peacemaking. Not so.

The Presbyterian church has stood up, repeatedly, through its statements and its representatives, to end those wars in the greater Middle East, to seek reconciliation with enemies and restoration for veterans, and to emphasize that without justice there can be no lasting peace. A faithful block of our congregations give steadily to our Peacemaking Program, and that program works both nationally and internationally. And a creative study process involving a wide range of our members helped to discern the "signs of the times" behind this book.

This book is written in the belief that God belongs in public discussion and that God's will for peace is part of the new creation of the world, which we see in the teaching, life, death, and resurrection of Jesus, the prophet from Nazareth. To use the word *Christ* is to see in Jesus' life a deep and cosmic pattern and purpose, not of God swooping in from outside but of God incarnate in the struggle, suffering, and ultimate triumph of love in the world we know. Or think we know.

To risk peace is to prepare to encounter evil and its power. One does not do this alone. The General Assembly itself—with the guidance of its social witness office—drew on the contributions of ninety-some congregations and presbyteries, the regional groupings of ministers and elders in our branch of Protestantism. One part of their discernment was to share—very carefully sometimes—personal experiences of war and violence. Veterans and survivors spoke: military folks, police officers, and protesters who have been beaten and jailed, people who know different sides of force and the courage nonviolence also requires. Very few people are untouched by violence, and few do not long for peace.

In the years of discernment, we saw nonviolent revolutions both win and get crushed. This book helps us to think about how and why that happened. Chris Iosso, the author, was the primary staff person and writer through the six years of discernment and has both unified and streamlined the full assembly language that is found on pc-biz.org, where all actions of each General Assembly are posted. I salute all of the voices he has brought together.

These recent years have also brought a new harvest of scholarship about Jesus as the organizer of a nonviolent reform movement as well as a prophet and more. This book distills some of that thinking, too.

So let us remember the Brief Statement of Faith (1991):

> In a broken and fearful world, the Spirit gives us
>   courage . . .
> to unmask idolatries in Church and culture,

to hear the voices of peoples long silenced,
and to work with others for justice, freedom,
    and peace.

I invite you to be both peacemakers and risk takers for the sake of the gospel.

J. Herbert Nelson II
Stated Clerk
General Assembly of the PC(USA)

Acknowledgments

My acknowledgements go first to all those who contributed to this project, key ones whom I have named in the dedication. The Advisory Committee on Social Witness Policy is more than an official body sustaining this and other work; it is a "consecrated" team of friends in service to Christ and the church. My war-veteran father and both grandfathers have also been present as I have drafted my own and edited the words of others. Peter Kemmerle, wise writer, and David Maxwell, a generous and equally wise editor, were critical in helping unite and clarify the voice of the book. And my chaplain wife, Robin Hogle, has brought home (in both senses) the reality of interpersonal violence as it is found in the emergency rooms and intensive-care units in all our hospitals. Our true enemies are not flesh and blood, but flesh and blood are what we have to hold and to heal, with God's help.

Introduction

Risking war is what nations often do. Risking peace is a task for the church. Jesus preached a kingdom where the lion would lie down with the lamb. His body, the church, must risk living that reign of peace. Nations can disregard the suffering of others. Christians cannot.

To risk peace means challenging the default setting of our society. And it means challenging ourselves. Christianity is above all a religion of love, a response by God to our universal longing for a new order of justice and blessing, as well as our response to God's call. What risks must we take for peace, and how do we help our country do the same?

The Presbyterian church has recently undergone a period of reflection on peacemaking. Building on past policy documents, people at all levels of the church studied and discussed what needed to be modified given the world context today. War is now waged differently than it was in 1998 when the church last gave in-depth attention to its vocation as peacemaker. Those who program the smart bombs and command the drones now wreak

1

devastation from a safe distance, but much of the world has not become safer. It is time the church evaluated whether its policies are able to address the demands of our day.

From 2010 to 2016, local churches, student groups, national conferences, and academics in the church debated, wrote, and decided on five affirmations the church must make to fulfill its peacemaking calling. Those affirmations become risks when truly taken, because their message collides with the demands for continued sacrifice by the powers that be.

This book does not minimize the violence that scars our species and steadily invades our souls. It contains biblical, theological, and historical insights, drawn from a discernment process of six years involving hundreds of people. Those participants were very aware of the impacts of fifteen years of war since September 11, 2001, the erosion of constitutional safeguards, and the tolerance—even preference—for new technologies of war, such as drones and smart bombs. A designated team of U.S. Christians with international experience helped streamline a broad set of learnings into the five basic challenges on which the chapters of this book are based.

Risking peace is not only about wars overseas. Gun violence, television and videogame violence, bullying, domestic violence, rape and sexual violence—in the military, and even in churches—are part of our culture. The realities of structural injustice and deprivation, of our being part of systems that exploit others, often beyond our awareness—these had to be part of our thinking and our prayer. Harsh, "weaponized" language in politics, sports, business, comedy, and on the Internet assaults our awareness, amplifying insecurity and fear. Economic and environmental disasters add to tensions among ethnic and racial groups. The seeds of peace are indeed beset by brambles and starved of good soil.

This book proposes five stages of creative resistance to violence. For members of the Presbyterian Church specifically, it offers next steps in a forty-year commitment to peacemaking. But for Christians and seekers more broadly, for U.S. Christians and citizens who are generally not pacifists, this book raises core spiritual questions. These address us individually and in the communities of faith and hope we desperately need. Peacemaking is a spiritual work, a calling, for all believers, and politics is only one of its forms.

In original format, these challenges were presented as a report to the Presbyterian Church (U.S.A.)'s 222nd General Assembly in Portland, Oregon, in June 2016. That report, called "Risking Peace in a Violent World," proposed a renewal of the church's witness to peacemaking, given the new reality of constant war. As guidance, it proposed that five "affirmations" be added to each congregation's commitment to peacemaking, and it offered a rationale for each one. Those affirmations and rationales—here called "risks"—offer a summary of recent Presbyterian thinking on our corporate calling to peacemaking. You could also say that these five commitments have been tested and found credible—precisely in faith terms—by a focus group of seven hundred people. The General Assembly, in fact, said the five in their initial form as a litany, moving from a call, through a confession of complicity, to a biblical summary, a charge, and a kind of doxology.

What we will see is that the General Assembly made some changes in the wording of the affirmations, changes that reflect the long debate within the church over whether pacifism or thorough-going nonviolence should be the church's own default position. Before we turn to the challenges—and the way that Presbyterian assembly focused them—let us put this debate in longer perspective, drawing on the wisdom of Presbyterian ethicist Ed Long.

The centrality of peace is a distinctive, biblical feature of Christian fidelity—especially in the idea of shalom in the Hebraic tradition and the idea of being peacemakers in the teaching and example of Jesus. However, translating these visions into policies that further human well-being has challenged Christian thinking ever since the church ceased to be bands of dedicated believers existing as outsiders within Greco-Roman culture.

Within the Christian movement two main traditions developed dedicated to the goal of peace, but each understood responsibility for achieving it in different ways. The first, claiming a strong grounding in the New Testament and the practices of the early church, is Christian pacifism; the other, the just-war tradition, grows out of the realization that when Christians become holders of authority and exercise office in a political world, they may be called upon to use violence for the protective love of neighbor and the maintenance of justice and order. We must be clear that both these moral stances are very different from the view that religion may use violent means to advance its own interests, as in crusades or holy wars. Yet the dangers of leaving war to the determinations of nation-states in the "modern" period are also clear: nationalisms and ideologies that still claimed de facto religious sanction for dominating others have been major causes of war for more than two centuries, particularly in Europe and countries colonized by European empires.

During the Protestant Reformation some groups, from which the "peace churches" emerged, understood Christian discipleship to require the repudiation of violence in the manner of the earliest church. Other groups, from which most mainline Reformed and Lutheran bodies emerged, understood Christian discipleship to allow for the restrained, and hence legitimate, use of the sword to preserve justice and order. Presbyterian confessions contain just-war positions in relation to the role of the "magistrate," or civil government. The criteria or conditions for a war to be justifiable are discussed in the fourth risk, but they are predicated on a preference for peace. War is an inevitably tragic last resort.

The just-war tradition grows out of the realization that when Christians become holders of authority and exercise office in a political world, they may be called upon to use violence for the protective love of neighbor and the maintenance of justice and order.

These two main Christian approaches to war and violence retained theological coherence as Christians sought to apply them through revolutions and wars of conquest, liberation, defense, and humanitarian intervention. American Presbyterians participated in and justified the Revolutionary War, the Civil War, World Wars I and II, and the Korean conflict but have been less and less of one mind on the more recent "wars of choice," such as Vietnam, the Nicaragua/Contra war, the two Iraq wars, and Afghanistan. The U.S. role in the Libyan and Syrian multiparty "proxy" wars raises additional questions addressed in the fifth risk (discussed in the fifth and sixth chapters).

Back in 1936 and 1938, when pacifist sentiment was strong in American Social Christianity, the General Assembly of the Presbyterian Church in the U.S.A. sent the presbyteries proposals to remove just-war language from the Westminster Confession, then the church's only confessional standard. While a majority of the presbyteries voted to remove or amend the language, in neither case did the outcome reach the supermajority of presbyteries required to accomplish that result. (Other churches also made pledges seeking to end war, driven by revulsion at the carnage in the trenches of World War I.)

During WWII, which had the overwhelming support of most Americans following Pearl Harbor, two important developments took place in the church. First, some Presbyterians felt called to be conscientious objectors and were generally supported (or at least benignly tolerated) in taking this position by the church. That support made it amply clear that a pacifist conviction was a legitimate form of Christian discipleship (which may reflect the influence of the votes in the 1930s). The second development was the Presbyterian church's work with other denominations to imagine a just and durable peace. Studies were undertaken in the denominations and ecumenical bodies exploring such concerns. That work contributed to support for the United Nations and the Universal Declaration of Human Rights and likely helped the postwar settlement avoid the vindictive features of the armistice that settled WWI.

The development of the Cold War—and its tendency to divide the world into two polarized positions—brought increasing questions about the wisdom and adequacy of military and particularly nuclear means for establishing peace and justice on a world scale. Many Christian ethicists argued that draft laws should recognize the validity of conscientious objection on just-war grounds as well as on fully pacifist grounds, and the General Assembly of 1967 emphatically reaffirmed the right of Presbyterians to be conscientious objectors.

This action highlighted the legitimacy of conscientious differences about participation in war by individuals and made individual integrity a foundational reference point for moral reflection. While the action did not overcome the differences between pacifist and just-war commitments in the church's corporate stand, it clearly undercut any presumption that just-war thinking inevitably means subservience to the policies of the state or that pacifism is unpatriotic.

Such was the situation when the church adopted the Confession of 1967, a bold declaration grounded in the idea of a shared church calling with strong social-ethical concerns for economic and racial justice, family life, and peace:

God's reconciliation in Jesus Christ is the ground of the peace, justice, and freedom among nations which all powers of government are called to serve and defend. The church, in its own life, is called to practice the forgiveness of enemies and to commend to the nations as practical politics the search for cooperation and peace. *This search requires that the nations pursue fresh and responsible relations across every line of conflict, even at risk to national security, to reduce areas of strife and to broaden international understanding.* Reconciliation among nations becomes particularly urgent as countries develop nuclear, chemical, and biological weapons, diverting their [hu]manpower and resources from constructive uses and risking the annihilation of [hu]mankind. Although nations may serve God's purposes in history, the church which identifies the sovereignty of any one nation or any one way of life with the cause of God denies the Lordship of Christ and betrays its calling. (*The Book of Confessions*, section 9.45; italics added.)

The first major policy statement on peacemaking to follow was *Peacemaking: The Believers' Calling* in 1980, which created the Presbyterian Peacemaking Program and which has the clear, simple, concise statement that "the church is faithful to Christ when it is engaged in peacemaking." This was followed by *Commitment to Peacemaking* (1983), signed by more than half the churches in the denomination. *Peacemaking: The Believers' Calling* was buttressed by significant additions in 1988, with *Christian Obedience in a Nuclear Age*, and in 1998, with the resolution on just peacemaking.

The recent history of our church is marked by a persistent belief in the importance of peace, but it is also marked by continuing good-faith disagreements as to what kinds of policies and commitments most faithfully translate that central belief into prudent and responsible, yet bold and inspiring action. Certainly the church has done laudable work in the thirty-seven years since *The Believers' Calling* was adopted, particularly in the extent to which it has managed to be critical of the prevailing trends in the society (of which it is an integral part). The Peacemaking Program published biblical studies, held conferences, and has influenced the vocabulary of the church. Yet the recent discernment process behind these five challenges was prompted partly by the fear that the program has been lacking in prophetic intensity during a time when the United States has been practically on a permanent war footing.

To address these concerns, the 219th General Assembly (2010) authorized a six-year discernment process to take a fresh look at peacemaking in the church's life, particularly the nonviolent understanding of Jesus' call to discipleship. A steering committee was appointed to devise opportunities for the broad membership of the church not only to consider the effectiveness of the church's peacemaking work but also to discern the basic nature and scope of the gospel's mandate for peacemaking.

Study documents were created and widely shared. Churches were consulted in 2013, and in 2015 presbyteries contributed an innovative kind of testing and confirmation received by few other statements of social witness. Military chaplains participated in the process. Professors and students from Presbyterian colleges and seminaries were consulted. Peace activists and Christian ethicists and biblical scholars were part of the peace discernment from the beginning.

The result of the thorough process was "Risking Peace in a Violent World." It recommended that the assembly adopt five affirmations to guide the peacemaking witness of the church into the second quarter of the twenty-first century. Though some wording was changed, the five affirmations that follow were approved, and the assembly retained the cases made for each in the full report. The five risks we propose here are thus guided by the wording of the assembly and also by the content of the full report.

1. We affirm that peacemaking is essential to our faith in God's reconciling work in Jesus Christ, whose love and justice challenge evil and hatred,

and who calls the church to present alternatives to violence.

2. We have sinned by participating in acts of violence, both structural and physical, or by our failure to respond to acts and threats of violence with ministries of justice, healing, and reconciliation.

3. We follow Jesus Christ, Prince of Peace and Reconciler, and reclaim the power of nonviolent love evident in his life and teaching, his healings and reversals of evil, his cross and resurrection.

4. Learning from nonviolent struggles and counting the costs of war, we draw upon the traditions of Just War, Christian pacifism, and Just Peacemaking to cultivate moral imagination and discern God's redemptive work in history. We commit ourselves to studying and practicing nonviolent means of conflict resolution, nonviolent methods for social change, and nonviolent opposition to war. Even as we actively engage in a peace discernment process, we commit ourselves to continuing the long tradition of support by the Presbyterian Church (U.S.A.) for our sisters and brothers who serve in the United States military, veterans, and their families. We promise to support materially and socially veterans of war who suffer injury in body, mind, or spirit, even as we work toward the day when they will need to fight no more.

5. We place our faith, hope, and trust in God alone. We renounce violence as a means to further selfish national interests, to procure wealth, or to dominate others. We will practice boldly the things that make for peace and look for the day when "they shall beat their swords into ploughshares, and their spears into pruning-hooks; nation shall

not lift up sword against nation, neither shall they learn war anymore."

The internal debate of the church is clearly visible in the second paragraph of affirmation 4, moving between its emphasis on nonviolence and language affirming the military and veterans (and presumably active soldiers) who still "need to fight." This book may help some readers make a more informed choice between strict nonviolence and a form of just war or just peacemaking. But it will fulfill its purpose above all if it helps the church be a more effective peacemaker, helping Christ "de-violence" all evils and turn all empires closer to God's commonwealth of peace.

Risk One

Commit to the Gospel of Peace

> We affirm that peacemaking is essential to our
> faith in God's reconciling work in Jesus Christ,
> whose love and justice challenge evil and hatred,
> and who calls the church to present alternatives
> to violence.
>
> Affirmation One, 222nd General
> Assembly (2016)

Peacemaking is at the core of our faith, not at the periphery. It's in our DNA. By not challenging evil and hatred, we disobey. The first risk is to take to heart the centrality of peacemaking to Christian faith and demonstrate what that faith looks like in practice, here, today. "The gospel of peace" is how the author of the letter to the Ephesians sums up the entire Christian message (Eph. 6:15). Another way to put this risk is that we recommit to reconciliation between ourselves and God, and between ourselves and other human beings. As Christians we can never give up on building relationships based on love and justice.

In 1975, the year the war in Vietnam ended, the General Assembly began a five-year study of the church's call to peacemaking. The policy statement that resulted was *Peacemaking: The Believers' Calling*, approved by the 192nd General Assembly (1980). That document offered a broad biblical, theological, and ethical basis for Christian peacemaking and also identified specific directions for that mission: efforts to reverse the worldwide arms race, "conversion of the economy from military to civilian production," and continuing attention to how justice relates to peace. It declared,

- The church is faithful to Christ when it is engaged in peacemaking.
- The church is obedient to Christ when it nurtures and equips God's people as peacemakers.
- The church bears witness to Christ when it nourishes the moral life of the nation for the sake of peace in our world.

The Believers' Calling led to the creation of the influential Presbyterian Peacemaking Program and established a special offering to fund it. It also broadened the concern for peace from being a matter of individual conscience and affirmed that peacemaking was the calling of all believers, particularly in light of nuclear and other Cold War dangers. Invoking Isaiah's vision of making plowshares from our swords (Isa. 2:4), it emphasized our global interdependence and international connection. With New Testament themes, it presented a holistic understanding of peace and encouraged a wide range of church engagement. It affirmed that "peacemaking is an indispensable ingredient of the church's mission. It is not peripheral or secondary but essential to the church's faithfulness to Christ in our time." Since 1980, peace-making has become broadly accepted in the church; it is integral to our prayers and hymns and is evident in our preaching, teaching, and public witness.

Presbyterians engage the gospel of peace in a variety of ways:

- Our worship points to the reality of God's gift of peace and mission of reconciliation.
- Through prayer we nurture the spiritual life of our communities.
- Through Bible study, we equip people to share the gospel message of peace throughout the world.
- We advocate for affordable housing, better schools, and funding for social services through faith-based community organizing campaigns.
- We work to reduce gun violence in the United States.
- We join with ecumenical and interfaith partners in struggles for human rights and economic justice in countries around the world.
- Presbyterian and ecumenical peacemakers risk nonviolent accompaniment, walking alongside church leaders threatened with political violence in Colombia, for example.
- We seek to make peace with the earth by living more sustainably.
- We challenge legislators to resist the pressures of special-interest lobbies and instead support forward-looking policies that reflect wise stewardship of the planet and respect for a more just world order.

Presbyterian Peacemaking Witness and Just Peace

Since the adoption of *The Believers' Calling* in 1980, careful studies and prophetic statements have addressed the nuclear danger, particularly military interventions and their rationale, and the relation of religion, violence, and terrorism. The Presbyterian Church (U.S.A.) has held a virtual "nuclear pacifist" position since 1988, opposing first use and retaliation and calling repeatedly for disarmament. The policy statement *Christian Obedience in a Nuclear Age* suggests that the Presbyterian Church (U.S.A.) takes a "just-peace" stance, with its images drawn primarily from the Old Testament:

> The church in the nuclear age must shift its energies from considerations of just war to the urgent and primary task of defining and serving a just peace. A nuclear stalemate or even the elimination of all nuclear arms is still far from God's shalom. Shalom is the intended state of the entire human race. It involves the well-being of the whole person in all relationships, personal, social, and cosmic. Shalom means life in a community of compassionate order marked by social and economic justice. Peace without justice is no peace; that is why the Bible so often reflects God's special concern for the poor and powerless.
>
> The great biblical visions of global peace—swords into plowshares, every family under its own vine and fig tree—are fundamental to thinking about just peace. Such a peace is ultimately God's gift; we need to avoid the proud illusion that we can create it by human effort alone. But Christian obedience demands that we move toward that peace in

all possible ways: by extending the rule of law, advocating universal human rights, strengthening the organs of international order, working for common security and economic justice, converting industry to peaceful production, increasing understanding of and reconciliation with those we identify as enemies, developing peacemaking skills, constructing concrete manifestations of just peace across barriers of conflict and injustice, and other means (*Minutes of the General Assembly*, 1988, pt. 1, 450).

In 1998, the assembly approved a statement called *Resolution on Just Peacemaking and the Call for International Intervention for Humanitarian Rescue* that embodied the tension involved in endorsing "humanitarian" military intervention as a method to prevent such things as genocide. The statement moves the church's thinking beyond the traditional categories of just war, crusade, and pacifism. Along with a realism that has been characteristic of much Reformed ethics (and some liberation theologies), the just-peace resolution affirms a preference for strong peacemaking initiatives, noting the following regarding the Presbyterian Church (U.S.A.):

It has called for greater emphases on the use of nonviolent means for conflict resolution and social change, and for the promotion of training toward this goal.

It has stressed the importance of human rights, religious liberty, and the importance of democracy as a foundation for just peace. . . .

It has called for the abolition of nuclear weapons, limitations on the development of weapons, and

Recent Presbyterian Peacemaking Statements

1967   *The Confession of 1967* honors peacemaking "even at risk to national security."

1969   "*War, Peace, & Conscience*" recognizes conscientious objection to particular wars as well as to all war.

1975   "*Ministry to Persons in the Armed Forces*" reviews and updates the role of chaplains to represent the independence and fullness of Christian beliefs on war.

1980   *Peacemaking: The Believers' Calling* sees all Christians to be peacemakers, across the range from nonviolence to the just-war tradition.

1983   "Commitment to Peacemaking," a widespread congregational pledge, included offerings for local, regional, and national programs and was supported by both of the reuniting Presbyterian churches.

1984–85   *Presbyterians and Peacemaking: Are We Now Called to Resistance*? is a widely studied resource challenging foreign interventions and the cold-war arms race.

1988   *Christian Obedience in a Nuclear Age* is a study and policy statement coming close to nuclear pacifism, mainly on just-war grounds.

1991	*A Brief Statement of Faith* includes the call to unmask idolatries and work for peace in "a broken and fearful world."
1998	*Resolution on Just Peacemaking and the Call for International Intervention for Humanitarian Rescue* states that military action may be justified to prevent genocide, yet ten key "just-peacemaking" principles would mainly prevent wars.
2004	*"Religion, Violence, and Terrorism"* recommends policing rather than a military model to deal with crimes of terrorism and stresses communal human security over national security.
2006	*"Resolution against Torture"* opposes excesses of U.S. occupations, reaffirms human rights, and calls for Guantanamo Bay prison to be shut down.
2010	*Gun Violence, Gospel Values* reports on gun proliferation and its effects.
2014	*Drones, War, and Surveillance* calls for drone and cyber security regulation, recognizing the pervasiveness of their use.

restrictions on the sale or transfer of instruments of destruction. It has supported these restrictions on the understanding that traffic in arms raises the likelihood of conflict and raises the level of violence should conflict break out. . . .

It has recognized the critical importance of racial and gender justice in the achievement of social harmony and prosperity.

It has called for independent and unilateral initiatives to reduce risks of conflict and to stimulate change. It has affirmed the importance of reconciliation even in the face of great risk. . . .

It has acknowledged the responsibility for international cooperation and leadership, and understands that the power and wealth of the United States require it to be part of international efforts to seek peace. At the same time it has recognized that the United States has and can abuse that power and wealth.

It has supported international efforts, through the United Nations, at peacemaking and peacekeeping. . . .

These church positions, together with background papers that support them, provide a complex legacy of important ideas. The Presbyterian church has not only made statements but has also encouraged participation in the ongoing tasks of peacemaking. Its peacemaking program has devised many strategies for helping to transform political and economic affairs in ways that promote just-peace policies, whether in the domestic affairs of our own nation or in the world at large, whether through the use of civil authority or, if needed, resistance to it.

In keeping with these principles and policies, General Assemblies have also called for responsible withdrawals by the United States from Iraq (2004) and Afghanistan (2010). The 2004 General Assembly prophetically and controversially termed the Iraq war "unwise, illegal, and immoral." The resolution on *"Religion, Violence, and*

Terrorism" (also 2004) endorsed a "policing" approach to terrorism and responds to the charge sometimes made that religion engenders violence. In 2008, the General Assembly "commended for study" a careful ethical assessment of the Iraq war titled "To Repent, To Restore, To Rebuild, and To Reconcile," which includes the concepts of public forgiveness and "honest patriotism" as developed by Donald W. Shriver Jr., a distinguished Presbyterian ethicist.

Recent theological discussion has proposed nonviolence for the majority of Christians as well, deliberately challenging the compromises seen to accompany public responsibility. The wording of the first of the five affirmations adopted by the General Assembly in 2016—the epigraph to this chapter—does not propose that nonviolence necessarily be an essential mark of the Presbyterian church, as it is for the traditional peace churches. Rather, it proposes that we have "a mission to present alternatives to violence." An earlier wording continued the sentence to include "fear, and misused power," underlining the breadth of reconciliation work and the possibility of constructive uses of power.

Our peacemaking approach must go beyond words and engage in transformative worship and action, creating needed alternatives for our society as well as ourselves.

Edward W. Long, a leader in Presbyterian peace thinking, has noted how today's pervasive acceptance of war's inevitability often becomes a self-fulfilling prophecy.[1] How does the church resist being transformed when it lives in a world of nations that are in constant overt and covert military struggle? This is where our peacemaking approach must go beyond words and engage in transformative worship and action, creating needed alternatives for our society as well as ourselves.

An updated Reformed approach was explored by a large number of congregations in the mid-1980s using the study guide *Presbyterians and Peacemaking: Are We Now Called to Resistance?*[2] That congregational process (and a parallel conversation among scholars virtually unique among denominations) generated some of the thinking about resisting violence that went into *Christian Obedience in a Nuclear Age* (1988). Some Presbyterians hold to fully nonviolent positions while a larger number argue that responding to injustice sometimes requires actions on the spectrum of force that include physical violence. During the six-year peace-discernment process, an overall consensus was reached to choose nonviolent alternatives whenever possible without making nonviolence an absolute position. The 2016 General Assembly went further than that, lifting up nonviolence and in a way heightening the risk or vulnerability of believers.

As we will see more in risk 3, it is important to consider nonviolence in relation to the example of Jesus and the witness of much of the earliest, pre-Constantine church. This is not to deny our traditional Presbyterian appreciation of how justice and love, like Old Testament and New, must always go together. According to biblical scholars Donald Gowan and Ulrich Mauser, the apostle Paul sees peace coming in *this* age, embodied in Jesus Christ and the redemptive work of the Holy Spirit. Peace is a key part of the hope of the gospel, part of what it is to live a redeemed and joyful life, larger than even the worst evils in history.[3]

Given this rich history of peacemaking and the vital ongoing work of making peace, it seems only fitting that we reaffirm the centrality of peacemaking and renew our dedication to this central calling as followers of Jesus Christ. At the same time, as an integral part of honest and authentic peacemaking, we must confess our complicity in the violence of our world.

Questions for Reflection

1. How do you personally embody peacemaking as a Christian in your life?
2. Do you believe there is a reason today for Christians to be absolute pacifists? Why or why not?
3. What alternatives to violence does/should the Presbyterian church offer the world?
4. How is the church at risk for presenting alternatives to violence?

Risk Two

Confessing Our Complicity

> We have sinned by participating in acts of violence, both structural and physical, or by our failure to respond to acts and threats of violence *with ministries of justice, healing, and reconciliation.*
> Affirmation Two, 222nd General
> Assembly (2016)

Making peace means engaging the critical issues of our times. Yet as those who are immersed in peacemaking know so well, faithful peacemaking must be spiritually rooted and sustained by the Holy Spirit. The heart and mind of the peacemaker must be liberated from conformity to culture and renewed in the mind of Christ (Rom. 12). This transformation is itself peacemaking work. John Calvin reminds us that the human heart is "a factory of idols." Therefore, healing the violence in our lives—not only the violence we do and the violence that is done to us but also our sinful capacity to accept it as normal—must be integrated into a holistic theology of peacemaking. The peacemaker must even confess the kind of complicity that comes from failing to avert violence even after great effort, a feeling shared by many who opposed the second Iraq war. Such awareness that we are all responsible for some measure of violence is an important admission of imperfection. In this section we move from an overview regarding violence in our culture and its structures to a closer look at the factors at work in the Iraq and Afghan wars in particular.

The commitment to peace that stands at the heart of Christian obedience requires that Christians take an honest look at the extent to which they are complicit in the violence that characterizes the society of which they are a part. This complicity is present despite good intentions to avoid it and worthy efforts to live by the ideal of peace. Identifying and confessing this complicity is difficult and painful work that is often sidestepped or ignored. This complicity has not necessarily come about through deliberate malice but inheres in the very course of living in an imperfect world where the human condition is marked by sin. If we fail to acknowledge our shortcomings, we only increase the probability we will perpetuate them. While nonreligious peacemakers may be mystified (or put off) by the idea of "the mind of Christ," taking the risk requires the spiritual virtues of humility and empathy to hear the cries of others and repent.

If we take a hard look at our society, we'll have to admit that violence has characterized much of our history and continues to dominate much of our current behavior. The American land in which we live was frequently taken from native peoples by force. The independence we value so proudly was achieved by a violent revolutionary war. Our national wealth was enhanced by the slave system that was abolished only with a civil war. We have profited from violence used to subdue workers and to control access to natural resources. It is hard to hear this kind of criticism of our country. The sting of such criticism may tempt us to falter when we confess our complicity. That's why we call this a risk. Christian patriotism, or love of any country, does not make of it an idol without flaws. We look for instruction from the Presbyterian church's Brief Statement of Faith, part of our *Book of Confessions*, which exhorts us to pray for the Spirit's courage to "unmask idolatries."[1]

We are addicted to violence for purposes of entertainment. Bullying is common in our schools, as is violence in our video games, murder mysteries, and crime dramas. The most popular sports often inflict injury, concussions, and trauma. Over 30,000 people are killed each year by guns, many of them suicides.[2] One in every four women in the United States experiences domestic violence during her lifetime.[3] We have stationed armed forces throughout the world on a quasi-permanent basis and defend ourselves with weapons that are used in the places where others live—often striking the innocent in the effort to destroy the guilty. A large segment of our economy involves the production and sales of armaments. And for many in politics, to apologize is blasphemy or betrayal, a sign of weakness rather than wisdom.

Structural Violence

Much of the hurt that is experienced in our society is produced by what is termed "structural violence," which contributes to many forms of oppression. A strict definition of *violence* is suggested by ethicist Mark Douglas: "a forceful action that intends to cause unwanted injury to another."[4] The adjective "structural" would modify this definition to "the operation of institutions and social structures that causes injury or deprivation to others." As we will see, systemic violence takes physical forms, even when they are not intentional or personal.

Our social and economic systems condemn a massive number of people to lives of poverty or fear—even when public investment and other measures could boost unemployment and raise wages. One fifth of U.S. children live in poverty,[5] one of the highest levels in the developed world. Concentration of ownership, regressive taxes, and wage stagnation have enabled the top 1 percent of Americans to reap between one fifth and one sixth of our nation's income in recent years and to have benefitted from almost all the gains of the economic recovery from 2009–2013, when the Affordable Care Act began to increase their taxes.[6] Workers overseas are paid much less and often endure far worse conditions to keep our prices low and top salaries high. An economy dependent on the burning of carbon fuels not only threatens our future but that of all other species. The purchasing of influence by corporations undercuts our democratic system. Physical assaults may not be involved or necessary in these processes, but they are nevertheless forms of violence.

A complete inventory of our complicity in violence is not in order here. That requires ongoing prophetic leadership, study, and moral inquiry. Christian communities must be constant and diligent in this task and be aware of likely resistance by some who will spread misinformation, distort arguments, and confuse real facts with myths. This kind of disciplined self-searching requires the capacity of the church and its members to transcend our own confining self-interest (as we know through our prayers of confession). Yet it is an essential aspect of being redeemed, of being transformed by grace. Society tends to honor the positive team player, the person who cheers on group activity with excitement and verve. When we affirm the need for confessing our complicity, we may prompt denial and hostility and be accused of negativity. To counter that normal human tendency is a vocation to heroic and prophetic humility without which the culture around us will never be healed. It is not easy to "unmask" the powers. We all wear masks to some extent and therefore need others to help us take them off. Those who embrace idolatries usually believe they are defending the truth. They—and we—need to hold a dialogue with those who differ from us, listening to them and hearing even the unspoken challenges to our views and unconscious ideologies. Discernment means prophetic criticism even of our so-called prophetic criticism. Yet confession, apology, and repentance can unlock the enormous powers of truth and love.

It is not easy to "unmask" the powers. We all wear masks to some extent and therefore need others to help us take them off. Those who embrace idolatries usually believe they are defending the truth.

With regard to that unconscious complicity, theologian Walter Wink believes we have embraced "the Myth of Redemptive Violence," the widespread belief that violence saves, that war brings peace, that might makes right. "The belief that violence 'saves' is so successful because it doesn't seem to be mythic in the least," Wink writes. "Violence simply appears to be the nature of things. It's what works. It seems inevitable, the last and, often, the first resort in conflicts. If a god is what you turn to when all else fails, violence certainly functions as a god. What people overlook, then, is the religious character of violence. . . ."[7]

From this perspective, violence is an idol, a false god. Violence does not save us from evil, sin, and death. It only adds to evil, sin, and death. As the Rev. Dr. Martin Luther King Jr. put it, "The ultimate weakness of violence is that it is a descending spiral, begetting the very thing it seeks to destroy. Instead of diminishing evil, it multiplies it. . . . Returning violence for violence multiplies violence, adding deeper darkness to a night already devoid of stars. Darkness cannot drive out darkness: only light can do that. Hate cannot drive out hate: only love can do that."[8]

To the extent that we have put our faith in violence instead of God, we must repent of our idolatry, for we cannot serve two masters. As Christians we confess that Jesus is our Lord and Savior, no other. Our security does not rest in violence but in God. Anthropologist Rene Girard argues that, on a deep level, the saving power of Jesus' life comes from his unmasking the way that spirals of violence create and condemn victims who are in fact innocent. Our discipleship, instead, commits us to an upward spiral that weakens the powers of domination.

The descending spiral of violence to which Dr. King referred often begins with structural violence—those social and economic structures that oppress and impoverish people, preventing them from meeting their basic needs and realizing their full potential. The structural violence of injustice and oppression can lead to the violence of revolt and rebellion that then leads to the retaliatory violence of government repression, which only compounds the structural violence of injustice and oppression and leads to further revolt followed by yet more repression. This is not to say that all violent crime in poor areas is a form of revolt but to say that those neighborhoods themselves are a form of crime against their inhabitants.

While direct physical violence is more visible and attracts more media attention ("If it bleeds, it leads"), structural violence is far more widespread and arguably does much more harm over time. We see it manifest in hunger and homelessness, poverty and disease. The processes of oppression noted above include patterns of inequality and exclusion called the "isms" of racism, sexism, classism, heterosexism, and ethnocentrism. These patterns operate at interlocking levels—institutional (policies and practices), interpersonal (group and individual), and cultural (social norms and valuing).

On one hand, most Americans know that the isms exist, but the common discourse in our country narrowly addresses only the discrimination that happens at the interpersonal level—when someone makes a blatantly derogatory comment or is accused of doing so. But even when a white police officer shoots an unarmed black teen, it is partly the conditioning of white privilege that heightens suspicion and pulls the trigger. On the other hand, most Americans may be unfamiliar with how the isms operate on this more insidious social level and unaware of their exacting toll. Yet millions of "lives of quiet desperation" are reflections of coercive inequality. We dehumanize ourselves and degrade others by unconsciously supporting patterns that pin our opportunities for well-being on our neighbors' marginalization. Structural violence militates against our Christian calling to be in authentic loving relationship with our neighbors, near and far.

Violence against the Earth

We are also doing violence to the earth and its creatures. The globalized economy is built on the untrammeled extraction of finite resources, the exploitation of cheap labor, and a no-limits-to-growth ideology, resulting in dangerously compounding climate change. We are destroying ecosystems, depleting precious natural resources, melting glaciers, raising sea levels, and causing a massive extinction of species as our greenhouse gases alter the ecology of the entire planet. Severe weather fluctuations are already causing tragic increases in hunger. In *Tropic of Chaos* (2011),[9] Christian Parenti warns that climate change is creating desperate refugees and the potential for serious violence in many regions. Resisting complicity here can mean bicycling or busing to work, investing in green technologies, and insisting on scientifically accurate reporting on the human impact on Earth's climate.

The Global Context for the Afghanistan and Iraq Wars

To confess our complicity in general without grieving for the two significant wars of the last fifteen years would be fairly painless. Yet to confess without addressing the underlying dynamics is too sentimental. Here we look briefly at the context for the Afghanistan and Iraq wars and then address the somewhat differing tragedies they embody. We return to the issues of U.S. superpower status in our discussion of the fifth risk.

From a global perspective, we who live in the United States are among the richest 20 percent of the world's population. (Consider that 40 percent of the world's people attempt to live on less than two dollars a day.) World income is distributed unevenly, with the top 20 percent of the world's people who live in the world's wealthiest countries receiving 83 percent of the world's income. The next 20 percent receive 10 percent of the world's income. The remaining 60 percent of the world's people share the remaining 7 percent of world income.[10]

Global economic inequality is nothing new. As far back as 1948, at the beginning of the cold war, George Kennan, head of the U.S. State Department planning staff, wrote the following in a secret policy-planning study:

> We have about 50 percent of the world's wealth, but only 6.3 percent of its population. . . . In this situation, we cannot fail to be the object of envy and resentment. Our real task in the coming period is to devise a pattern of relationships which will permit us to maintain this position of disparity. . . . To do so, we will have to dispense with all sentimentality and day-dreaming; and our attention will have to be concentrated everywhere on our immediate national objectives. . . . We should cease to talk about vague and . . . unreal objectives such as human rights, the raising of living standards, and democratization. The day is not far off when we are going to have to deal in straight power concepts. The less we are then hampered by idealistic slogans, the better.[11]

How do we "maintain this position of disparity"? What does it mean to "deal in straight power concepts"? Thomas L. Friedman, the foreign affairs columnist for the *New York Times*, explains it this way: "The hidden hand of the market will never work without a hidden fist—McDonald's cannot flourish without McDonnell

Douglas, the builder of the F-15. And the hidden fist that keeps the world safe for Silicon Valley's technologies is called the United States Army, Air Force, Navy and Marine Corps."[12]

Though there were multiple sources of our country's original wealth, our privileged economic position is preserved through U.S. military power as well as through military aid and weapons sales to governments around the world. Even though it is a violation of U.S. law, the weapons we sell to foreign governments are sometimes used by their militaries against their own people in order to maintain a stable environment for corporate investments. Militarization makes corporate-led globalization possible. Whether militarization itself is finally profitable is one of the questions that Afghanistan and Iraq raise.

The Iraq and Afghanistan Wars

Since the terrorist attack on September 11, 2001, involving four hijacked civilian airplanes and approximately 3,000 civilian casualties, the United States has been engaged in two significant wars, a limited intervention in Libya, various forms of military assistance in Syria, and drone warfare in a number of other countries—all under the same initial authorization of force. The war in Afghanistan has been a joint operation with NATO member armies, as was the military intervention in Libya. The war in Iraq was initiated without United Nations authorization and involved a "coalition of the willing," with Great Britain most notable among the U.S. allies. The General Assembly's calling the Iraq War "unwise, immoral, and illegal" clearly invoked just-war teaching, which says that in order to go to war certain conditions must be met. Preemptive

---

Summary of Just-War Principles

Principles that apply to the decision whether or not to go to war (*jus ad bellum*):

1. There must be just cause.
2. There must be right intention.
3. The action must be undertaken by the proper authority.
4. The action must be taken as a last resort.
5. There must be a reasonable hope of success (to defend, protect, or otherwise gain a just peace).

Principles that apply to the conduct of war (*jus in bello*):

1. The force or violence used must be proportional to the result intended.
2. Noncombatants are not to be directly attacked.

---

war was seen as antithetical to last resort; nonexistent weapons and regime change were not seen as just cause; unilateral action spurned the legitimate authority of the U.N.; and while military success was assured, a military occupation seemed unlikely to achieve the goals of democratization or a just peace.

The Iraq and Afghanistan wars have been extremely costly in both human and economic terms. The numbers of Afghans, Iraqis, and Pakistanis who have died in the fighting are conservatively estimated to be 210,000.[13] Our repentance must include the long refusal of our occupation forces to count those deaths. Their survivors face many of the same issues that U.S. war veterans do, but without the medical and social support. War refugees from Afghanistan, Syria, and Somalia alone totaled 8.7 million out of 65.3 million people displaced overall at the end of 2015, according to the U.N. High Commissioner for Refugees.[14] More than 6,800 U.S. soldiers have been killed, and more than 52,000 have been injured in Afghanistan and Iraq, where U.S. troops went back in after the so-called Islamic State or ISIS surged in 2014.[15] Multiple deployments have put enormous stress on U.S. soldiers and their families, whose lives have been changed forever by the experience of war. Even after soldiers return home, war continues to take its toll through unemployment, domestic conflict, depression, alcohol and drug addiction, post-traumatic stress disorder, moral injury, and suicide.

The Iraq and Afghanistan wars will cost the United States alone an estimated 4.8 trillion dollars, when current and future veterans' costs are added up.[16] The costs of far less extensive military activity by other countries involved is considerably less,[17] and U.S. costs for activities labeled reconstruction (but often security-related) have been estimated about $130 billion in Afghanistan and about half that in Iraq as of 2015.[18] Actual reconstruction of Afghan and Iraqi homes and infrastructure would be another figure entirely. Most Americans now question whether these military interventions have been worth the enormous cost in lives, national treasure, and reputation, particularly as it is not at all clear what they have achieved. This adds to an "increasing sense of the impotence of military might" and the belief that "the main problems of the world will not yield to military solutions," as *The Believers' Calling* puts it.

A case can be made that disproportionate militarization is undermining the U.S. economy and creating additional structural violence or oppression. While weapons manufacturers posted record profits during the deep recession of 2008–2010, our cities and states are often in a state of fiscal crisis; public services and welfare programs, especially for our more vulnerable citizens, continue to be slashed; and the federal debt due to war remains high. We will say more about the "military industrial complex" in our discussion of risk 4. The money used each year to prosecute the war in Afghanistan could fund the Head Start program for the next fifteen years, but instead many U.S. children will grow up with an inferior education. With the money spent in Afghanistan, we could provide health coverage to every American, thereby, according to a Harvard study, saving 45,000 American lives in one year. The budgets for the wars in Iraq and Afghanistan could fill the budget gaps in all the states, preventing deep cuts in programs to the poor, the sick, and the uneducated.[19]

The money used each year to prosecute the war in Afghanistan could fund the Head Start program for the next fifteen years, but instead many U.S. children will grow up with an inferior education.

When we chose between the ability to kill militants and civilians on the other side of the globe and the ability to provide for the health and education of our children, it was a moral decision. Instead of spending 700 billion dollars simply for a decade of business systems modernization, for example, a program that Secretary of Defense

Gates shut down for having only marginally enhanced our military capability, we could have chosen to invest in infrastructure or green energy. This was a moral choice, and it was the wrong one, even if that example is a small amount for the Pentagon.

In the 2010 General Assembly debate over the resolution to call for withdrawal from Afghanistan, six years after the church had called for an end to the Iraq war, it was claimed that the strategic goals for the 2001 invasion had been met: Al Qaeda leaders had been dispersed or killed, and the military capacity of the Taliban had been downgraded. To stay longer was to accumulate enemies and support a corrupt government without adding much to regional or global security. Those judgments may be criticized, but the church accepted a stronger initial justification for the Afghanistan war than was the case in Iraq. Yet our moral accountability as a nation in both countries has to do not only with the invasion and occupation but the final cease fire and the future prospects for those nations. If Iraq is any indication, those prospects are not good. While our preeminent military role in the world does not make us accountable for all world problems, these two wars will be very hard to defend before the bar of history and history's Judge.

The risk in this chapter is to acknowledge and understand the interlocking web of violence in our lives, our society, and the world, and then to call the church to confession. War and oppression are closely intertwined. Engaging violence in ourselves and in the structures of our society and our world is essential to the integrity of our faith, yet daunting, complex, even overwhelming. With a spirit of repentance, then, we turn back to the heart of our faith.

Questions for Reflection

1. What idols of violence do you see around you?
2. List three to five ways you are complicit in violence. What would you risk if you actively unmasked your own complicity? Can you be a strict pacifist while participating in structural violence?
3. Where do you see the myth of redemptive violence—the belief that violence saves—being propagated in your life?
4. Which of the peacemaking policy statements found in the text box are you familiar with? Which would you like to find and read?
5. Write a brief prayer of confession for complicity in violence, ideally including personal and corporate participation.

Risk Three

Reclaim Christ the Peacemaker

We follow Jesus Christ, Prince of Peace and
Reconciler, and reclaim the power of nonviolent
love evident in his life and teaching, his healings
and reversals of evil, his cross and resurrection.
Affirmation Three, 222nd General
Assembly (2016)

The Life and Teachings of Jesus

Since the Presbyterian church and other churches mobi-
lized for peace and against nuclear war in the 1980s,
there has been another kind of mobilization: of historical
scholarship about Jesus of Nazareth. While this scholarship is enormously varied and involves a wide range
of early Christian texts, it offers the church much rich
reflection on the interaction of Jesus, the peasant population, the Jerusalem authorities, and the Roman army.
Prominent scholars in these studies include Marcus
Borg, N. T. Wright, Walter Wink, Elisabeth Schüssler

Fiorenza, Elaine Pagels, John Crossan, John Meier, and Richard Horsley. Jewish and Muslim scholars have added their volumes to this mix. The studies have found a clear preference for nonviolence in the example and teaching of Jesus. Even those who emphasize Jesus' engagement in confrontation and conflict rarely link him to violent revolution.

To "*re*claim" Christ as peacemaker is to *again* place special emphasis on Jesus' nonviolent movement and methods and to remember the example of the early church. Before Constantine, the early Christian communities were more likely to endure violence than to exercise it. Though our churches are not in the persecuted and socially marginal position of the early church, we still need to be a lot clearer about who we are and what weapons we fight with. In this chapter we will look first at recent interpretations of Jesus and then propose ways that new emphases and learnings can strengthen future Presbyterian peacemaking theology and formation.

Let us first heed the biblical scholar Luke Timothy Johnson, who reminds us that our faith is not in the result of any scholar's interpretation. Johnson insists that the canonical collection of literary texts called the New Testament is united in witnessing to the meaning of the Jesus story and that meaning is found in a pattern consistent with the cross and resurrection: "Jesus' existence as one of radical obedience toward God and self-disposing service toward others forms a pattern for all humanity that can be written in the heart by the Holy Spirit. It is this pattern that Paul designates as the *nomos Christou* ('the law of Christ,' or, better, 'pattern of the Messiah')."[1] The first question, then, is whether peacemaking or nonviolence is part of that basic pattern.

Without attempting a full survey, we compare now several very different scholarly approaches to Jesus and violence, beginning with the work of Richard B. Hays in *The Moral Vision of the New Testament* (1996):

> Matthew 5:38–48 . . . teaches a norm of nonviolent love of enemies. . . . Do the other texts (than Matthew) in the canon reinforce the Sermon on the Mount's teaching on nonviolence, or do they provide other options that might allow or require Christians to take up the sword? When the question is posed this way, the immediate result—as [Karl] Barth observed—is to underscore how impressively univocal is the testimony of the New Testament writers on this point. The evangelists are unanimous in portraying Jesus as a Messiah who subverts all prior expectations by assuming the vocation of suffering rather than conquering Israel's enemies.[2]

Of the letters of the apostle Paul, Hays chooses to lift up Romans 12–13, noting that "though the governing authority bears the sword to execute God's wrath" (13:4), this is not the role of believers. As Paul's military metaphors make clear, "the weapons of our warfare are not fleshly" (2 Cor. 10:4). Hays sees the book of Revelation not as ferociously violent but as a counsel to endurance. Texts that seem to allow for violence, such as Jesus' "cleansing" of the Temple, Hays sees as a series of prophetic confrontations: "From Matthew to Revelation we find a consistent witness against violence and a calling to the community to follow the example of Jesus in accepting suffering rather than inflicting it."[3] For Hays, the greatest challenge is the disjunction between his New Testament understanding of nonviolence and the witness of the Old Testament, which he thinks could provide the only possible scriptural bases for the just-war and holy-war traditions.

For contrast, we turn to Richard Horsley, a biblical scholar with a sociological starting point, who sees Jesus more focused on achieving justice than peace. Horsley's analysis shows Jesus leading a social movement that challenged the social order as much as it sought to reform Israel's religious life. Nonetheless, Horsley states,

> Jesus, while not necessarily a pacifist, actively opposed violence, both oppressive and repressive, both political-economic and spiritual. He consistently criticized and resisted the oppressive established political-economic-religious order of his own society. Moreover, he aggressively intervened to mitigate or undo the effects of institutionalized violence, whether in particular acts of forgiveness and exorcism or in the general opening of the kingdom of God to the poor.[4]

Horsley considers injustice to be a form of structural violence. He sees Jesus as primarily a prophet out to renew a religious and social covenant. In the cultural context of the first century, where religious and political allegiances are deeply entwined, Jesus demonstrates nonviolent resistance to a host of malevolent powers, particularly in the Gospel of Mark. Although some of Jesus' parables contain moments of climactic judgment, the reign of God is more about voluntary social solidarity than violent end-of-the-age events (eschatology). While Horsley downplays things like an apocalyptic second coming, he stresses the dramatic importance of the crucifixion.

Walter Wink sees in Jesus "a third way" that resists evil through nonviolent means, an approach that outflanks and subverts aggression, sometimes by one's choosing to suffer. From this perspective, turning the other cheek, offering more clothing than a coat, and going the second mile are examples of the weaker party taking the moral initiative and humanizing the opponent, forcing him or her to recognize one's own humanity without resorting to violence. It is a strategy with social and cultural implications, potentially breaking cycles of subjugation and humiliation, exposing injustice in power dynamics, and neutralizing and undermining the threat of violence.

From this perspective, turning the other cheek, offering more clothing than a coat, and going the second mile are examples of the weaker party taking the moral initiative and humanizing the opponent, forcing him or her to recognize one's own humanity without resorting to violence.

Wink's interpretation is a way of accounting for a prophetic and nonviolent life that posed a clear alternative to the domination systems of his time, though it does not deny the violent imagery in some of Jesus' parables. Wink presents a Jesus of inner power who, when a Samaritan village refused to host him, refuses his disciples' idea "'to command fire to come down from heaven and consume them'" (Luke 9:54). Jesus rebukes them, saying, "'You do not know what spirit you are of, for the Son of Man has not come to destroy the lives of human beings but to save them'" (Luke 9:56, manuscript variant b, NRSV). Similarly, when Jesus exorcizes evil, it can be seen as his engaging with violent forces. Exorcism is more commonly understood as a kind of healing that may involve spiritual convulsion; it undoes or disarms the violent spirits from those possessed. In peace scholar Andrea Bartoli's words, exorcisms are not so much nonviolent as "de-violencing."[5] Jesus's actions may not fit a specific contemporary definition of *nonviolence*, but his willingness to face conflict was never a willingness to choose violence.

Of Jesus' death on the cross, Martin Luther King Jr. said, "Jesus eloquently affirmed from the cross a higher law. He knew that the old eye-for-an-eye philosophy would leave everyone blind. He did not seek to overcome evil with evil. He overcame evil with good."[6] "Those who want to save their life will lose it," Jesus says, "and those who lose their life for my sake, and for the sake of the gospel, will save it" (Mark 8:35). Jesus's life of "radical obedience toward God and self-disposing service toward others,"[7] led to the cross. Those who wish to be disciples of Christ know what to expect if they pick up the cross and follow Jesus (Matt. 16:24). Yet Christians also live in the hope that death does not have the final word. The "pattern of the Messiah" articulated by the apostle Paul involves not only sacrifice. It also holds out the promise of resurrection and new life.

The Example of the Early Church

Besides the life and example of Jesus Christ we also have the witness of the early church to guide us. Most early Christians in Rome refused to engage in violence, trusting that their love for fellow citizens would point people to the new day dawning in Jesus Christ. Yet some, like the early theologian Tertullian (circa 155–240 CE), seemed to be less concerned with violence itself than the fact that soldiers were required to participate in the emperor cult. Others, like Tertullian's near contemporary Clement of Alexandria, noted that when soldiers converted to Christianity, they were not always asked to change their profession. Still the early church largely made a nonviolent witness and suffered frequent martyrdom.

There is no affirmation of killing or war in the writings of the early church, nor is there the idea that Christians making war would make the world a better or safer place. Thus we find prohibitions against killing of any sort, some of which even denied the Eucharist to persons who engaged in such acts.

Those early Christian theologians who made a strong nonviolent witness also read the Hebrew Scriptures through the lens of Christian faith. They took with utter seriousness the prophecies of Micah and Isaiah, asserting that the Messiah had indeed come, and that the time had come to enact their prophecies of beating their swords into plowshares and their spears into pruning hooks (Mic. 4:3). They did not interpret the violence in their Scriptures (i.e., the Christian Old Testament) as giving them license to kill. Indeed, there is no affirmation of killing or war in the writings of the early church, nor is there the idea that Christians making war would make the world a better or safer place. Thus we find prohibitions against killing of any sort, some of which even denied the Eucharist to persons who engaged in such acts. The early Christians were known not to watch killings, either by viewing legal executions or by attending gladiatorial games. In sum, then, while there is some scholarly debate over why the early Christians avoided violence and whether it reflected their marginal social location, the general witness is clear.

In the fourth century, the church's relationship to the Roman Empire and to violence changed. The Roman emperor Constantine converted to Christianity in 312 CE and began promoting the faith instead of persecuting it. By 380 CE, Christianity had become the state religion. During this period, Christians started to take up arms. The change was such that while in 303 CE it was generally forbidden for Christians to serve in the military, by 416 CE only Christians were allowed to serve.

During the transition period, Christian reflection on the wars of the Roman Empire contributed to the creation of the just-war doctrine, which was initially articulated by Bishop Augustine of Hippo based on ideas of Bishop Ambrose of Milan and the Roman philosopher Marcus Tullius Cicero (106–43 BCE). The just-war approach established the ground rules under which a Christian might be understood to be acting morally—out of love and hence sorrowfully—even when killing other human beings. Augustine meant to protect civilian populations in a time when the Roman Empire was falling into disorder, which accounts for the tradition's emphasis on defensive war and, what is often lost, right intention. "Peace as the harmony among people is the theme of Augustine's great philosophy of history in the *City of God* . . . ,"[8] and order more than power is what is desired from the empire or its representatives. Later just-war theories, such as that of Thomas Aquinas, are based more on reason and justice concepts such as "natural law" and, for good or ill, can function apart from Christian faith. (A list of the just-war principles are on page 34.)

Implications of Jesus and Early Christian Nonviolence

It makes a difference whether one sees Jesus as nonviolent or not, but it does not automatically imply that our discipleship should or could be the same as his calling, nor that we should seek martyrdom or withdrawal to the desert following a model from the earliest centuries of our faith. Some Christians see Jesus laying down nonviolence as an absolute rule, for example, and others see him upholding an ideal. To take the third risk—to "reclaim" Christ the peacemaker—is to wrestle with or discern personally where one stands on nonviolence in relation to Jesus Christ. The witness of the first Christian centuries is important as well, both to help interpret Jesus Christ and to illuminate our current context.

The Old Testament is the broader guide to our understanding Jesus and, indeed, to our reading human history. Drawing on hundreds of years of Hebraic experience with God, it develops a moral vision that shaped the rabbi Jesus and many of the New Testament writers.

With the Old Testament comes the need to interpret the violence attributed to God and that attributed to human beings, and to do that in relation to newer views of Jesus. Those views, as we have seen, show him avoiding violence but not conflict, seeking reconciliation with justice, and resisting evil by yielding to God in such a way that the theologian Albert Curry Winn called him the original "reverse fighter."[9] The third risk—of reclaiming Christ the peacemaker—requires new thinking for the church, such as Jerome F. D. Creach's *Violence in Scripture* (2013), which in response to portrayals of Jesus like that of Richard Hays above wrestles with the bloodiest texts about conquest, holy war, vengeance, hell, and judgment.[10] Overall, we see scholars distinguishing God from "the wrath of God" and recognizing the ways that evil misdirects and corrupts power when it can. God uses but does not give value to violence.

A temptation for those of us influenced by Christian realism is to use the Old Testament in our peacemaking literature only for its counterexample of a wrathful God. This is untrue to the Old Testament, which also gives us visions of shalom, rules to restrain evil, and prophecies of a new covenant, as in Jeremiah 31.

Much of the traditional Reformed reading of pacifism was that it was impossibly perfectionist and entailed renunciation of power (as in priestly vows) or withdrawal from the world (in monasteries or in sectarian communities like those of the Anabaptists). It may have worked for the early church, so that thinking went, but they were not powerless and on the margins by choice. Jesus' teachings were sometimes considered impossible ideals or a short-term ethic in anticipation of an imminent end of the world. Here we suggest that better-argued interpretations of Jesus' mission and his "reversals of evil" can help renew our peacemaking witness.

At the same time, it is clear that faithful resistance has a force to it, and thus nonviolence itself can be a form of coercion. Daniel Ott states this explicitly in "Toward a Realistic, Public, Christian Pacifism," arguing that "a realistic pacifism must be a pragmatic pacifism that acknowledges that even physical coercion may in a few instances be necessary as a result of our 'responsibility to protect.'" Yet for Ott, even in policing, "nonviolent strategies are morally superior . . . through the ability of nonviolence to engage in conflict while honoring the moral primacy of human life."[11]

The Context of Empire

Two final observations may help us in reclaiming or renewing our understanding of Jesus the peacemaker. The first has to do with the context of empire for most of the Old Testament and for the early church. The Hebrew people were first enslaved by and then liberated from the Egyptian Empire. The nation of ancient Israel was conquered first by the Assyrian Empire and later by the Babylonian Empire. Eventually, the Judeans living in exile in Babylon were allowed to return to Jerusalem as a result of the expansion of the Persian Empire. And the entire New Testament takes place in the context of a Roman Empire supported by conquest and slavery. Both John the Baptist, the last of the great Hebrew prophets for Christians, and Jesus of Nazareth, the One to whom he pointed, called for repentance, proclaiming the reign of God. They spoke of the reign of God as an alternative social order based on a rival set of values to those of the Roman Empire. Here is the choice put before the early Christians, imagined in contemporary preaching style:

> For all its monumental cultural achievements, the Roman Empire was a system of domination; the Reign of God on the other hand, is a domination-free order. The Roman Empire was based on economic exploitation; the Reign of God is based on economic justice. The Roman Empire was based on violent pride; the Reign of God on nonviolent love. The Roman Empire projected a matrix of iron-fisted control; the Reign of God sings the songs of freedom. The Roman Empire was built on layers of oppression; the Reign of God is founded on the

hope of liberation. The Roman Empire's brutality struck fear in its subjects; the Reign of God offers the balm of healing. The Roman Empire promised peace through victory; the Reign of God promises peace through justice.[12]

In fact, the Roman Empire continued in several forms after its "fall," and empire continued as a sometimes aspirational category in Europe even after the Treaty of Westphalia 1648 began to formalize nation-state sovereignty. More will be said about empire as a tendency or temptation in risk 5, part 1.

The second observation has to do with the social and cultural location of the mainline Protestant church today. In comparison with past levels and positions of influence for ecumenical Protestant leaders in the culture, many see a trend toward marginalization. Another word used is "disestablishment." Our numbers are smaller, and although many politicians are practicing, mainline Christians, secularization consigns religious institutions to the private sphere of values. Thus the church's public voice is taken less seriously and is distinctly unwelcome in some quarters, including much of the academy. This is not to argue that religion or Christianity is without influence in what is still a highly religious country, but it suggests that we are in a pluralistic situation somewhat closer to that of the early Christians.

While our relative minority situation may well be cause for lament and deep concern, it may, paradoxically, free the church from the burden of straddling two worlds and serving two masters. From this standpoint, for centuries the church has spoken in a "Constantinian dialect," that is, speaking both as followers of Jesus Christ grounded in his message and values *and* as stewards of the social order caring for the interests of the nation or empire. This is an opportunity—still in service to the common good—to make sure we witness to God's uncommon good, which we see in the power of nonviolent love in the Christ story.

If Paul and the Pauline communities can be taken as guides, the early Christians focused on the distinctive practices and values of their faith first, but with a genuine concern for their larger communities. In Victor Paul Furnish's analysis, Paul wanted people "not . . . conformed to this world, but . . . transformed" (Rom. 12:2) yet still to behave "noble in the sight of all" (Rom. 12:17).[13] The world was passing away—an apocalyptic element is there in Paul's letters, and Christians are already citizens of a heavenly commonwealth (Phil. 3:20). But they are not "transients" or "resident aliens," not in Paul's language.[14] The early churches are not concerned about institutions per se, but they are concerned to discern what is moral in the places they are set and "work for the good of all" (Gal. 6:10) and "live peaceably with all" (Rom. 12:18).

The charge that ecumenical Protestantism is "irrelevant" often reflects an effort to weaken its voice when we argue that patriotism does not mean automatic approval of military ventures.

The core of the risk of reclaiming Christ the peacemaker, then, is not to be compromised in maintaining structures that perpetuate violence, as can happen when we imagine more influence than we have. Our call is not to preserve privileges but to resist pressures that would make the church a junior partner to nationalism. The mainline churches have been influential when they have taken prophetic positions. The charge that ecumenical Protestantism is "irrelevant" often reflects an effort to weaken its voice when we argue that patriotism does not mean automatic approval of military ventures.

More than that, though, reclaiming the nonviolence in Jesus of Nazareth makes it harder for God and God's church to be co-opted. It changes our "default" setting and rebalances our approach to the Old Testament. What this means in practice leads us to the next two risks.

Questions for Reflection

1. The Jesus as portrayed in the Gospels always actively opposed violence. Do you? Why or why not?

2. Several prominent scholars' ideas about Jesus' approach to violence are mentioned in this chapter. Which most appeals to you? Why?

3. What are the implications for the church given that we follow a savior who opposed violence?

4. How might the marginalization of the mainline church free it from serving two masters?

5. How is following this Jesus a risk?

Risk Four

Practice New Peace Strategies

Learning from nonviolent struggles and counting the costs of war, we draw upon the traditions
of Just War, Christian pacifism, and Just Peacemaking to cultivate moral imagination and discern God's redemptive work in history.
Affirmation Four, 222nd General
Assembly (2016)

The fourth risk Christians must take is to choose peace
through justice rather than peace through strength. We
looked at some of the causes of war and violence in risk 2,
confessing our complicity in the ways injustice is "baked
in" to global inequalities, causing suffering and resentment in too many places. The argument here is not sim-
plistic. We should learn from all the ways Christians and
others have sought to restrain and end war. But our case
for new peace strategies is that they make new communications and global trends work against oppression and
that they refuse to accept old moral compromises that
have weakened our ecumenical witness. Thus, while evils

still abound, our faith takes the form of moral imagination so that we risk claiming that God is still at work in history, redeeming the time set before us.

In the language of our popular culture, this chapter is about how to end zombie wars and the zombie thinking—or brain eating—that allows them to continue. Its focus is mainly international, though nonviolence training and communication have relevance to U.S. civil rights and public protest matters noted in risk 2.

Along with new insights from Jesus scholarship summarized in risk 3, new Christian thinking about peacemaking must take into account the series of substantially peaceful transitions that have occurred since the fall of the Berlin wall in 1989. These include other transitions in Eastern Europe and the disintegration of the Soviet Union itself; a cessation of terrorism alongside the implementation of power sharing in Northern Ireland; the massive demonstrations that led to the end of the Marcos dictatorship in the Philippines (after the killing of Benigno Aquino); the still-surprising end of apartheid in South Africa, including the Truth and Reconciliation process; and the initial successes of the Arab Awakening in Tunisia and Egypt, where dictatorships collapsed with great speed. As continuing developments in Egypt underline, in no case does justice or democracy simply fall from heaven. Yet these notable cases are part of a larger picture presented by scholars in which nonviolent regime change is approximately twice as successful as violent government overthrow.[1]

The counterexamples of Syria and weakened or collapsed states such as Somalia, Mali, and parts of Congo illustrate the combined powers of disorder, sheer repression, climate change (all around the Sahara desert), and cross-border extremism, sometimes funded by neighbors more interested in proxy wars than collective security. Certainly the pictures of tortured bodies and videos of beheadings show the depth of evil and dehumanization. The continued violence in Iraq and Afghanistan reflects, in part, the failure of military intervention to ensure either democratic institutions or equitable development. In Syria, the 2013 decision of the United States and other Western powers to pull back from air strikes on the regime in exchange for chemical weapons disposal and peace talks was initially claimed as a triumph for both threatening intervention *and* for multilateral negotiation. Russia's intervention in 2015, partly to protect the Christian minority in Syria, and the so-called Islamic State's threat to dictatorships and democracies alike, point to the need for peace negotiations with all nations involved, across ideological and sectarian divides. Such negotiation in relation to Iran's nuclear program bore fruit in a well-structured agreement in 2015, arresting their efforts at bomb making, lifting some sanctions, and allowing Iran to participate in efforts for a Syrian peace agreement.

These real-world cases demonstrate that international relations are complex and that the churches, to offer credible witness, need to have the capacity for analysis as well as a passion for peacemaking. In this section we first present emerging nonviolent strategies that are clearly preferable to continued dictatorships protected by short-sighted alliances, commercial interests, and massive weapons sales. We note the contributions made by just-war and just-peacemaking strategies and their limitations (see the just-war principles on page 34). This section concludes with the claim that the church's capacity to nourish the moral life of the nation (a goal of the 1980 *Believers' Calling*) depends on its ability to nurture a moral

Six Elements of Nonviolent Strategy

1. Nonviolence is for the strong rather than the weak. It is a difficult discipline that eschews cowardice. It is not nonresistance but a particular method of resistance.

2. Nonviolence does not seek to "defeat or humiliate" the opponent but to win them over. It is not employed for the purpose of scoring points but as a means of creating "the beloved community."

3. Nonviolence directs itself "against forces of evil rather than against persons who happen to be doing evil." One may despise a particular form of evil, but one may not despise the doer of the evil.

4. Without making suffering into something to be sought, nonviolence can bring home the truth that "unearned suffering is redemptive." It can be creatively enacted in ways that transform evil into a potential for good.

5. The attitude of nonviolence must be within the heart of the individual as well as in his outer actions. "The nonviolent resister not only refuses to shoot his opponent but he also refuses to hate him."

6. Nonviolence "is based on the conviction that the universe is on the side of justice." The practitioner can believe that she is not going against the grain of what is ultimate but seeks rather to exemplify what is ultimate: redemptive suffering love.*

*Martin Luther King, Jr., *Stride toward Freedom: The Montgomery Story* (Boston: Beacon Press, 2010), 90–95.

imagination willing to take risks for peace and envision new relationships.

Nonviolent Direct Action and Nonviolent Ethos

Nonviolent direct action, best known from the work of Mohandas Gandhi and Martin Luther King Jr., has proven to be an effective means of wielding power in a variety of conflicts. It is the source behind the previous examples: the nonviolent "people power" that freed the Philippines; the pro-democracy movements in Poland, East Germany, and Czechoslovakia that ousted communist regimes in 1989; and the antiapartheid movement in South Africa, supported by international economic pressure, that brought an end to white minority rule. Lesser known cases are the nonviolent student movement in Serbia that ousted a weakened Slobodan Milosevic in the year 2000 and the peace achieved in Mozambique with the assistance of Roman Catholic mediators. Christians participated in these movements for social change, using methods of nonviolent action reminiscent of the civil rights movement that changed the United States.

Nonviolent direct action—the use of protest marches, strikes, boycotts, sit-ins, and more—is a means of wielding power and a technique for waging conflict, just as guerrilla warfare, conventional warfare, and terrorism are also means of waging conflict. Nonviolent direct action is distinct from some methods of conflict resolution in that it seeks to surface, escalate, or intensify conflict. It does *not* require its practitioners to be committed to a philosophy or ethic of nonviolence so long as they follow the methods and stay united. Indeed, people often choose nonviolent action for pragmatic reasons rather than religious, moral, or ethical ones. In this way, strategic nonviolence counters one argument sometimes made against religious nonviolence or Christian pacifism: that it fosters a nonengagement or withdrawal, a search for uncompromising purity, in the manner of Amish communities, Jehovah's Witnesses, certain Catholic orders, or some forms of Buddhism or Jainism

Nonviolent, people-power movements have shown themselves capable of overthrowing dictators, thwarting coups d'état, defending against invasions and occupations, challenging unjust systems, promoting human rights, and resisting genocide. A recent study, "Why Civil Resistance Works: The Strategic Logic of Nonviolent Conflict," by Maria J. Stephan and Erica Chenoweth, compared the effectiveness of violent and nonviolent resistance campaigns in conflicts between nonstate and state actors between 1900 and 2006.[2] The study found that "major nonviolent campaigns have achieved success 53 percent of the time, compared with 26 percent for violent resistance campaigns." Jesus' third way of nonviolent action may not work in all circumstances, but the historical record shows that its contemporary analogues are a powerful means of engaging in conflict and can be used successfully in struggles for justice, human rights, and self-determination.

The work of nonviolence theorist Gene Sharp, *From Dictatorship to Democracy*, was often used as a manual during the Arab Awakening. Widely translated and reprinted, it contains practical guidance for assessing the weak points of repressive governments and building movements, along with a list of 198 nonviolent methods. Sharp's strategy would suggest, for example, that though the Syrian protesters were right to try nonviolent means at first, they had not prepared enough of the population for the regime's response and the influx of extremists pursuing a proxy war. Though Sharp stresses the pragmatic applicability of nonviolent strategies to struggles anywhere, we are particularly interested, as Christians, in relating them to our "world-transformative" ethos and motivating hope.

Nonviolence may be thought of as both an end and a means. It is an end insofar as it refers to the future world for which we long—a world free from violence and war, free from hunger and poverty, free from injustice and oppression, and full of God's love, justice, and healing. We may understand it as Jesus' "kingdom of God" or Martin Luther King Jr.'s "beloved community," or Walter Wink's "domination-free order." Leo Tolstoy's reading of Jesus in the Gospels influenced Gandhi in finding the *satyagraha* ("truth force") in his religious tradition. Henry David Thoreau's civil disobedience is an example of nonviolence as an ethic or applied philosophy of life. As an ethic, it has often been disparaged as a form of withdrawal or an attempt to escape complicity in life's power struggles. Certainly parts of the Mennonite tradition reflect that withdrawal. Quakers, while declining to be public office holders in the past, now are often deeply and tenaciously engaged even with government policies they oppose. This shift in outlook is not about withdrawal but about being willing to suffer out of love. The paradigm for this is the well-known story of the Dutch Mennonite, Dirk Willems.

These alternative visions and actions contribute to the church's witness by framing it as a "contrast model" to more violent, hierarchical, or competitive social relations. Nonviolence and pacifism need not be based solely on a personal ethic of imitating Jesus. A nonviolent communal ecclesiology can involve clear beliefs about every member sharing in the gifts of the Spirit, which include peace. The contrast model grounds peaceful resistance to evil both in God's interaction within individual human

The Dirk Willems Story

Dirk Willems was a Mennonite in the city of Asperen in the Netherlands. He was captured and imprisoned for the "crime" of being rebaptized, of allowing secret church services in his house, and of letting others be baptized there.

Knowing that he would be put to death if he remained in prison, he made a rope of strips of cloth and escaped from prison. A guard chased him. Shortly, Dirk ran across a pond covered with a thin layer of ice. He made it, but his pursuer fell in and would have died. . . . Knowing the risk, Dirk turned back and pulled the man to safety.

Dirk Willems was returned to prison and put to death days later, May 16, 1569.

conscience and within dedicated, worshiping communities. Personal and collective forms of nonviolent action are described later in this book as "'things that make for peace,'" (Luke 19:42), but ideally they are rooted in the life of the church.

What if the Presbyterian Church (U.S.A.) reoriented more of its common life around the Prince of Peace? What if we reemphasized the nonviolent example of his life and witness in our preaching and teaching, our spiritual formation and worship, and our public witness in our violent world? Would many of our congregations and those of other "mainstream" Protestants be comfortable seeing themselves as countercultural alternatives?

Many Presbyterians have rarely given serious attention and reflection to questions of violence and nonviolence, war and peace. With some exceptions for the racial-justice struggles in the United States, people in the pews have seldom heard these subjects addressed in sermons, nor have they talked about them in Christian education classes. Many participants involved in discussing the Presbyterian church's peacemaking policies recently reported that it was their first introduction to the ideas of Christian nonviolence. At the same time, many were also unfamiliar with the actual content of the just-war and just-peacemaking approaches. Leaders must do a much better job of teaching peace to people in the pews.

Just-War Principles

We have mentioned the just-war tradition at various points (see the list on p. 34). Retired Presbyterian chief of chaplains Kermit Johnson applied its categories of ethical decision to nuclear war. He concluded that even various "tactical" or limited nuclear war scenarios could not be justified.[3] Just-war principles shape even some pacifist thinking—for example, in the Presbyterian Church (U.S.A.)'s adoption of a nearly "nuclear pacifist" position. In light of St. Augustine's insistence on right intention, ethicist Ronald Stone has argued that the threat of "mutually assured destruction" could not be justified.[4] The Roman Catholic Church took another stance in 1983, during the cold war, when the bishops' pastoral letter "The Challenge of Peace" accepted deterrence conditionally (but indefinitely), saying it was not "adequate as a long term basis for peace."[5]

The Presbyterian General Assembly's opposition to nuclear war in *Christian Obedience in a Nuclear Age* (1988) was also based partly on just-war criteria, as was its critique of the Iraq war (2004). The clear implication of the church's stand against the Iraq "war of choice" is to rule out the purported doctrine of "preemptive war" practiced by the second Bush administration in the absence of a real or imminent threat. Indeed, if the six-year process of discernment revealed any consensus on a specific policy, it was to oppose preemptive war, possibly even if the other side actually had weapons of mass destruction.

The just-war tradition is intended to serve as a constraint on the use of military force—to minimize the violence used in achieving a particular objective. *All five* criteria must be satisfied if military action (*jus ad bello*) is to be considered morally justifiable: just cause, right intention, proper authority, last resort, and reasonable hope of success. Once a nation has committed to military action, that conduct (*jus in bello*) must adhere to two additional criteria—proportionality and discrimination (avoiding noncombatants).

Though we have seen the utility of just-war criteria as a means of assessment, their flexibility is often exploited by those seeking war or defending the necessity of certain war practices. Critics question the practical value of just-war criteria if they do not give clear direction to decision makers about which course of action is more moral. Some in the Christian realist camp of Reinhold Niebuhr challenge the "natural law" bases of just war (such as the claimed right to self-defense) and doubt that war can ever be a rational or fully rule-governed activity.

A case in point: World War II, the so-called "good war," is widely considered to have been a "just war." However, it did not meet all of the criteria of a just war. U.S. involvement in the war was certainly prompted by just causes—responding to the Japanese attack on Pearl Harbor and countering the aggression of Nazi Germany in Europe. But the conduct of the war devolved into "total war" with both sides bombing cities indiscriminately,

killing hundreds of thousands of noncombatants, cul-
minating in the U.S. atomic bombing of Hiroshima
and Nagasaki in pursuit of unconditional surrender and
possibly to signal Russia. The 158th General Assembly
(1946) responded: "Christians know that war is evil. The
use of the atomic bomb means that war reaches a degree
of destruction which multiplies this evil beyond human
concept." The assembly went on to call for "immediate
cessation of the manufacture of atomic bombs."[6]

Despite the elasticity of just-war criteria, as long as U.S.
military actions are presented as morally justifiable based
on those criteria (whether or not there is a declaration of
war), it is important that Presbyterians be well-versed in
this tradition so that they can participate intelligently in
the public debate and not be deceived by national leaders bent on using military force. The 1988 *Christian Obedience in a Nuclear Age* statement recognized that most
acceptance of war is based not on just-war thinking but
on *unthinking* obedience to the state and political forces;
hence various means of resistance were seen as consistent
with Reformed teaching.

The most important approach to the just-war tradition
that has evolved in post–World War II ethical thinking
is to emphasize how the preference for nonviolence can
orient the just-war criteria. This understanding is aug-
mented in the just-peacemaking preventive measures that
build on the principle that war is a last resort. Resort to
violence in war, as many in the military as well as civilian victims know, is inevitably tragic and frequently
means suspending moral criteria in the name of survival.
Christopher Hedges, a former war correspondent (and
Presbyterian minister), has also illuminated the virtually
addictive thrill of combat violence.[7] This is far from the
right intention enjoined by just-war proponents.

Ten Principles of Just Peacemaking

1. Support nonviolent direct action.
2. Take independent initiatives to reduce threats.
3. Use cooperative conflict resolution.
4. Acknowledge responsibility for conflict and injustice and seek repentance and forgiveness.
5. Advance democracy, human rights, and religious liberty.
6. Foster just and sustainable economic development.
7. Work with emerging cooperative forces in the international system.
8. Strengthen the United Nations and international efforts for cooperation and human rights.
9. Reduce offensive weapons and weapons trade.
10. Encourage grassroots peacemaking groups and voluntary associations.*

*See Glen Stassen, ed., *Just Peacemaking: Ten Practices for Abolishing War* (Pilgrim Press, 1998).

Just Peacemaking

What the just-peacemaking principles do well is to introduce a whole new body of practical measures for conflict resolution and reconciliation forged in some very difficult circumstances, often with strong Christian inspiration. Two examples of peacemaking explicitly focusing on forgiveness are Fr. Leonel Narvaez's School of Forgiveness and Reconciliation in Colombia and elsewhere in Latin America, seeking to help heal the effects of "dirty wars," and the work of political scientist Donna Hicks on ways to restore dignity to victims of violence and humiliation.[8]

What the Presbyterian church and other U.S. Christian bodies have not done fully or effectively is to provide a moral analysis of certain major developments in war making. These include the near abdication by Congress of its power to declare war; the movement of many combat functions to private contractors and voluntary enlistees, which makes war a profit-making enterprise; and the development of sophisticated weaponry in robotics, nanotechnology, drones, and more. Cyberwarfare introduces further issues, as it can both disable digitally controlled defenses and repurpose communications devices, exploiting political and psychological tensions within opposing militaries and their larger societies. Hacking elections, as Russia has been accused of doing, adds another dimension to international competition and contention.

The Church and the Military

As long as Presbyterians continue to serve in the U.S. military, the Presbyterian church has a responsibility to care for active-duty soldiers, veterans, and their families. Our denomination does this by providing chaplains to the military through Presbyterians Caring for Chaplains and Military Personnel (PCCMP). An influential essay by a current chaplain, Captain Mel Baars, discusses her ministry in Afghanistan after September 11, 2012: "[The mission of these ministers is] to provide military personnel with a visible reminder of the HOLY in the midst of combat and chaos."[9] Chaplains serve as noncombatants; they are prohibited from carrying firearms. They offer worship, prayer, and Bible study, and they spend much of their time providing pastoral care and counseling to the soldiers in their units. Chaplains also may serve as a moral voice on the battlefield, where life-and-death decisions are being made daily. Chaplains are often the only ones in the chain of command who can hear and hold the terror of young soldiers facing death and the remorse a soldier feels in taking the life of another human being. Chaplains themselves carry a large burden in being present in war, as enemies who are also made in the image of God are objectified and killing becomes routinized.

Chaplains themselves carry a large burden in being present in war as enemies who are also made in the image of God are objectified and killing becomes routinized.

This last task is especially critical given the decades-long decline in mainline Protestant participation in the military chaplaincy, especially since many who have been drawn to military chaplaincy have been influenced by syncretistic theologies that combine God and American exceptionalism. Indeed, military training is designed to break down the innate reluctance to take the lives of our fellow human beings and to make killing, even under limited circumstances, normative and necessary. Furthermore, war doesn't end when the deployment is over; its lingering effects continue long after veterans—including chaplains—return home.

Our congregations also have a role to play in supporting military families while their loved ones are deployed overseas and after they return home. Multiple deployments put enormous stress on soldiers and on the spouses and children they leave behind. Even when soldiers return physically unscathed, parts of the soul can remain on the battlefield. This can mean depression, suicidal thoughts, and post-traumatic stress disorder, which are sometimes exacerbated by public doubts about or lack of support for the wars. Veterans need the love and care of congregations who will welcome them home and listen to them with wisdom. The church has a special responsibility to help heal the moral and spiritual wounds of its sons and daughters who have been scarred by war. For instance, in the Greek Orthodox tradition there is a ritual cleansing from the spiritual defilement of violence. A new approach to the "moral injury" of war has been pioneered by Rita Nakashima Brock and Gabriella Lettini, working with retired army chaplain Herman Keizer.[10]

The PC(USA) also has a responsibility to its youth and young adults to help them examine their own consciences and to work through the ethical arguments for serving in the military versus declaring oneself a conscientious objector to war. Young people are presented with these important decisions early in their lives. We fail them if we do not equip them to make these decisions faithfully and wisely.

Developing the Moral Imagination

John Paul Lederach, a Mennonite veteran of peace building, has mediated conflicts for the last thirty years. Lederach identifies the moral imagination as the capacity to imagine and design processes within the real-life challenges of violence without being caught up in destructive patterns:

> If we are to survive as a global community, we must understand the imperative nature of giving birth and space to the moral imagination in human affairs. We must face the fact that much of our current system for responding to deadly local and international conflict is incapable of overcoming cycles of violent patterns because our imagination has been corralled and shackled by the very parameters and sources that create and perpetuate violence.[11]

The moral imagination is activated when "politics as usual" fails to deliver, and it requires the capacity to risk a new world. This risk is embedded in three related capacities: to imagine ourselves in a web of relationships in which all parties are knit together, to embrace the complexity of every conflict, and to act creatively, especially given the risks it takes to imagine peace. Peace building requires that people be able to envision their interconnectedness and mutuality. Daniel Ott emphasizes how peacemakers must see that real change is possible and not be stuck in fatalism, determinism, or an inevitable dualism of church versus world. Without the inner strength of hope, Christians would not have led in the struggles to abolish slavery, honor women's equality, pay workers fairly, protect the rights of children, or fight global warming today.

Moral imagination also involves the capacity to rise above polarities of "us and them" and divisions of "with us or against us" and reach beyond accepted meanings. "Paradoxical curiosity" is the gift of respecting complexity and of searching beyond the visible and discovering unexpected potential. To risk is to step into the unknown without guarantee of success or safety. For many people caught in conflict, violence is the known, and peace is the mystery. Because peace building typically requires people to move toward a new, uncertain, and unexpected future, it can be a difficult journey. Yet Christ clearly calls us to join him in risking peace and transforming conflicts by boldly practicing the "'things that make for peace'" (Luke 19:42).

Moral imagination is thus our greatest ally in taking the risk of practicing new peacemaking strategies, whether or not we are entirely convinced of the necessity of nonviolence. Increasing evidence suggests that nonviolence can be very effective—but it is not for the faint-hearted. In risk 5, part 1 we look at the morality, legitimacy, and effectiveness of war from the position of a superpower. Without understanding how to use past tools like the just-war criteria, we are even less able to resist automatic political cheerleading for war and military solutions. Human security is more fundamental than national security, and it has to do with the character of our communities. This is why the church must risk and be brave enough to confront a violent culture and embody alternatives to it.

Questions for Reflection

1. Define *moral imagination* in your own words, and give an example if you can.
2. Where do you get your news? How do you evaluate its reliability?
3. Where have you witnessed nonviolent direct action? Name ways it can be effectively used today.
4. How can church leaders teach peace to people in the pews?

Risk Five, Part One

To Convert the Empire (Again!)

> We commit ourselves to practice the things that
> make for peace in our daily lives, families, and
> communities, to risk calling our nation back
> from the practices of empire to the highest ideals
> of our heritage, and to take part in social move-
> ments for a domination-free order.
>
> Initial proposed language, Affirmation Five,
> 222nd General Assembly (2016)

As followers of Jesus Christ, we are called to seek first
the kingdom of God. Peacemaking is part of our seeking
that reign or commonwealth where God's will is done on
earth as it is in heaven. Until that day, prophetic discipleship involves risk, and we hope this challenge is faithful to
the risk involved. This chapter begins with our Christian
vision of "things that make for peace," then outlines the
scale of those "practices of empire," and concludes with
ideas for scaling up our peace practices.

The doxology-like charge at the end of the next chapter
is the language the 2016 General Assembly finally adopted

as its fifth affirmation, and it is a partial description of what opposing empire means, based on renouncing the use of violence, at least in pursuit of selfish national interests. Although many Presbyterians are uncomfortable with naming our own country an empire, we keep the original language here because it properly states the challenge and need for social movements beyond the church to help in the conversion we pray for. Before we get to that Great Day when "[God] will wipe [away] every tear" (Rev. 21:4) and "the leaves of the tree are for the healing of the nations" (Rev. 22:2), we will need to take many smaller steps and oppose fearful nationalism at many points. The language of empire is also part of the Accra Declaration of the World Communion of Reformed Churches, which identities it as a set of interlocking power relationships.

By taking the fifth risk, we do not seek to put our country's national security in jeopardy but to enable the church to contest the way our nation has extended its understanding of national security into its relations with the rest of the world. During the last fifteen years of wars, since the relative peace of the 1990s, there has been a stepping back from real leadership in creating world order. Between the reptilian social brain of empire thinking and the idea of a "domination-free" order modeled on the kingdom, there is a distance that communities of faith must help our country navigate. When fears of the other are stoked, when national glory is understood primarily in terms of power, when terrorism is magnified, when presidential candidates compete in threatening war crimes, then the church (like the prophets) must call the nation-state back, in our case to liberty and justice for all and to hopes that America would be an exception to old-world power politics. Even though the church itself will never become that domination-free order, it remains our vision for measuring all the orders in which we live.

To practice in our daily lives the things that make for peace requires love, consideration, and respect for others and the laws that keep our communities peaceful. We count on the disciplines of faith: prayer, worship, and self-awareness in relation to Christ's Spirit present with us. There are disciplines of communal life that we learn in the church—from not letting the sun go down on our anger to understanding that we all have different gifts to use for the common good. The first four risks we take for peace do not put us into conflict with our citizenship or ask us to critique the international relationships our government pursues. The fifth risk—attempting to convert the empire—challenges us to recognize that, as beneficiaries of past inequality and continuing privilege, we are complicit with structural violence. We acknowledge that nations do not behave as individuals, yet we hold to our deepest hopes of peace with justice. Our dispositions and our disciplines can be much strengthened in this direction.

Our confirmation and adult education classes can teach forgiveness, reconciliation, and conflict resolution as practical strategies, and our public witness can look more wisely and critically at the national interests we are called to fund or defend. To meet this challenge is not only to seek to be nonviolent in our own lives but to seek to reorient our society away from the lure of empire and its structures of domination toward the promotion of a sustainable global community in which basic human needs are met and security assured for all people. That goal is not utopian; in environmental terms, it is past the time to end the waste of war and focus on climate change.

It is clear, after more than fourteen years of war, that a majority of Presbyterians are deeply concerned about the enormous human and economic costs of war—the hundreds of thousands killed in Iraq and Afghanistan, the millions of people displaced by the violence, the thousands of U.S. soldiers killed or injured, the trillions of dollars spent, and the damage done to our economy. A majority of Presbyterians are also deeply worried about the pervasive violence in U.S. culture—seen in gun violence, sports, entertainment, and our tolerance for hunger, poverty, abuse, and neglect. As we seek to be just and loving in our own lives and in our congregations, so as Reformed Christians we believe the church is called to invite the nations of the world into new understandings of how to respond to violence in our time. The church is called by the Scriptures to be a countercultural community, as it was in its first three centuries of growth, pointing the world to God's coming reign in Jesus Christ. The times cry out for the church to bring forward the Spirit's healing and transformational gifts in new ways.

> The church is called by the Scriptures to be a countercultural community, as it was in its first three centuries of growth, pointing the world to God's coming reign in Jesus Christ.

Don't Confuse the Cross and Flag

Use of the concept of empire was opposed by some in the presbyteries that responded to an earlier version of the document approved by the 2016 General Assembly. We understand that definitions of *empire* differ, that the United States is not the only empire, and that empires come in several kinds. For some, *empire* is a pejorative term for "Babylon," which in Revelation bears "the mark of the beast," a stain of evil. It names the misuse of power, the use of other people and nations for our benefit more than theirs. Others, such as John Ikenberry, maintain that America does not generally relate to the world as an empire (that is, as a sole power with client states), but when it acts outside of international institutions, as in Iraq, it loses moral legitimacy. For still others, *empire* is not a pejorative term. They think that without some system of international order the world would devolve into a global failed state and that empires should be judged by their approximation of Christian and human values. Consider the Roman Empire, for example. For all its faults, after the fall of the Roman Empire literacy virtually disappeared, and it was another 1,000 years before one could freely travel from Great Britain to Egypt.

We'll use the idea of empire to address the purposes of power in this chapter, and we'll look at the differences between national security and human security, by which we mean *safety and sustainability of life provided through cooperative action to meet human needs.* The Presbyterian peacemaking calling means helping our nation change its orientation to the world from that of a superpower to something less grandiose. No one sees the United States losing its military preeminence any time soon or can yet articulate a realistic alternative ordering of international security, but true national strength would have our country be "number one" again in some other measures of national achievement than military strength. Currently we rank nineteenth in the world, well behind much of Europe and Asia in indicators of social well-being and even wealth, when public goods and education are factored in.[1]

The fifth risk lifts up a vision of God's reign of justice and peace as an alternative to power relations predicated *primarily* on force. The United States does not stand above the inevitable competition among nations seeking their own interests. China, Russia, and other major powers maintain empires through trade, alliances, and force. Ethnically different sections of some countries may be controlled by majorities and even internally colonized. Our role remains dominant, however, despite the tragedies of Iraq and Afghanistan, and the interests for which we sustain our massive military presence around the world remain largely unquestioned. Do alliances with warlords or religiously exclusivist states really defend our freedom and preserve security, or do they undermine it? It is honest patriotism to challenge U.S. foreign and military policies that try to dominate the rest of the world in order to maintain our "American way of life" at the expense of others. It is a matter of Christian discipleship to minister to those who are dominated by any power, and this requires us always to be clear about who "we" are: Christians and citizens who do not confuse the cross with the flag.

Colonialism, Empire, and Postcolonial Empire

The early church stood largely in opposition to the practices of the Roman Empire, though it could also be grateful for the way Roman roads and free travel allowed evangelists to carry the gospel to distant locales. Christians naturally did not believe that emperors were divinities and were sometimes persecuted for their disbeliefs. This changed in 380 CE when the Roman Empire officially adopted Christianity as the state religion, beginning a long symbiotic relationship between the church and Roman Empire.

The Peace of Westphalia (1648), which followed the repeated breakup of would-be successors to the Roman Empire, created a system of nation-states that recognized one another's sovereignty. These European states expanded into global empires and colonized other lands. They often did this with the de facto blessing of the Catholic Church, sometimes with the formality of the papal "doctrine of discovery." Explorers and conquistadors conquered lands and peoples with Christian missionaries in their wake. This was true of the Spanish, the Portuguese, and the French, with some variation for the reconfigured Protestant monarchies of the British and the Dutch, shown in the range of settlements in the Western Hemisphere starting in the sixteenth century. Elsewhere in the world, powerful nations such as the Ottomans exercised their power to control the land and resources of others in a variety of ways, often settling regions, dispossessing native inhabitants, and imposing new languages, cultures, and religions. Following the disruptions of World Wars I and II, newly independent colonies sought to join the Westphalian community of nations as instituted in the United Nations. Even after independence, though, many nations maintained relationships of dependency with the former colonizers.

In the case of the United States, original hopes of being a New Israel took new forms on the frontier, and manifest destiny led to wars of conquest, however rationalized. Following World War II, the United States led the way in creating numerous international institutions such as the United Nations, NATO, the World Bank, and the Bretton Woods Agreement. These institutions were to follow the rule of international law and enhance human rights. The high ideals of these institutions were soon overtaken by the cold war, which pitted the forces of global communism against the free world under the leadership of the United States. In this bipolar world, the United States dominated countries indirectly by supporting military dictators, such as Marcos in the Philippines, the Somozas in Nicaragua, and the shah in Iran. We extended our influence and leverage by providing governments with military and economic aid. With military equipment came training and enduring relationships with foreign militaries, whatever their human rights records. Where there has been resistance to U.S. influence—whether it be in Cuba, Nicaragua, or Iran—the United States has reacted with military and economic force.

The collapse of the bipolar world created by the cold war (1989) left a unipolar world, with the United States possessing the strongest military and largest economy, unchallenged anywhere in the world. Shortly after the collapse of communism, the United States, working with NATO, helped to bring peace to the conflict in the former Yugoslavia. Then, working apart from international institutions, in violation of international law, and ignoring the counsel of many allies, America invaded Iraq, a move that greatly undercut America's moral legitimacy even among those who supported us. We have thus increasingly faced limits in the projection of American power, not only in our inability to influence the direction of countries we invaded and/or occupied but in the rise of regional powers (i.e., China and Russia) and the region-wide influence of Islamic extremism (as in the so-called Islamic State). Though these dynamics test the United States' position as the sole global leader, it is fair to say that Pax Romana has become Pax Americana.

Difficult as it may be for Christians living in the United States today, it is incumbent upon us to recognize that we live in what many consider the heart of empire (in the pejorative sense). This is so even in our own faith community, the World Communion of Reformed Churches. WARC's Accra Assembly (2004) stated, "In using the term 'empire' we mean the coming together of economic, cultural, political and military power that constitutes a system of domination led by powerful nations to protect and defend their own interests."[2] The Accra Declaration (often called the Accra Confession) criticized the unregulated or "neoliberal" market system in ways that were prophetic in light of the credit crash of 2008. The declaration's larger claim was that economic globalization was strengthening inequality among and within nations, to the benefit of those at the top of a hegemonic order. We may not think easily about empire, but that's part of the point. As Americans, we don't think twice about the United States maintaining approximately 750 overseas military bases in 130 countries. Imagine some other country wanting to operate a military base on U.S. soil!

But like Jesus, John the Baptist, and the Hebrew prophets before them, the church today has a prophetic calling. As the body of Christ, the church continues the work of Christ in the world. We have a responsibility to speak truth to power, to challenge the status quo, to be a voice of conscience to our nation and to the world.

Given the freedom and prosperity most Presbyterians experience inside the United States, we don't often challenge the status quo. If we raise our voices in opposition to U.S. empire, we may not speak very loudly. But like Jesus, John the Baptist, and the Hebrew prophets before them, the church today has a prophetic calling. As the body of Christ, the church continues the work of Christ in the world. We have a responsibility to speak truth to power, to challenge the status quo, to be a voice of conscience to our nation and to the world.

Aspects of Empire in U.S. Policy Today

Three crucial statements of U.S. foreign and military policy have been made since 1980: the Carter doctrine, the Powell doctrine, and the Bush doctrine. The Carter doctrine says that the U.S. government reserves the right to use military power to guarantee access to Middle East oil. The Powell doctrine expressed the U.S. aspiration to "full spectrum dominance," that is, the ability of the U.S. military to bring dominating military force to bear on any situation anywhere on the planet. The Bush doctrine, with its embrace of "preemptive and preventive action," claims that the U.S. government has the right to "defend" itself against putative or imagined threats by striking adversaries preemptively. All three of these foreign-policy strategies rely on a military role and can be termed "militarism." Particularly during the second Bush administration, our military sought capacity to operate three different war theaters at once. Though the Obama administration criticized the Bush doctrine, it did not articulate a doctrine for its own increasing reliance on drones and special operations forces.

It is important for us to recognize how far these developments depart from the U.S. Constitution's opposition to a standing army and from historical practice in which the size of the U.S. military corresponded to the immediate threat or task to which it was directed. Since the end of the cold war, the size and capability of our military has taken on a life of its own, independent of any specific threats. Americans had grown to see it as their right and responsibility to police the world; powerful interests benefited from this. Then the terror attack of 9/11 occurred, prompting a virtual doubling of military and surveillance expenditure even independent of the two wars, which were funded by debt.

Today our nation's ability to project armed force beyond our borders is second to none. We have the best-trained and best-equipped armed forces in the world, and we spend more on our military than do the countries with the next ten highest military budgets combined. The United States is by far the largest arms dealer in the world. U.S. foreign military sales surged in 2014 to a record $36.2 billion, accounting for over 50 percent of the global arms market.[3] The U.S. military budget is larger than all other federal programs except Social Security. The United States retains a network of military bases around the world from which to project force, carry on surveillance, and protect oil and other resources. U.S. military intervention had become relatively normal since the end of the cold war—in Haiti, Somalia, Bosnia, Kosovo, the Persian Gulf—and then Afghanistan and Iraq II opened new horizons, including Pakistan, Yemen, Libya, and various military assistance operations in the western hemisphere. Hardly a year has passed without a significant military action. Living in a state of war has become the rule rather than the exception.[4]

National Security has become the overarching interest with which the United States approaches the world. Since

"the war on terror" began, covert operations, surveillance, and drone missiles have taken on a central role. The
growth in the U.S. intelligence community has been stag-
gering. According to a July 2011 series in the *Washington
Post* called "Top Secret America," some 1,271 government
organizations and 1,931 private companies then worked on
programs related to counterterrorism, homeland security,
and intelligence, with an estimated 854,000 people holding
top-secret security clearances.[5] The threat of terror is not
to be dismissed, but that label may conceal the way that
covert operations (such as providing arms, training, and
surveillance data) destabilize traditional societies and how
globalization creates cross-border networks of grievance.

Perhaps more important, our nation's engagement
with the world is becoming more militarized. U.S. military forces are being increasingly asked to do things that
have until now not been considered part of their job—
for example, nation building, which had been handled by
international diplomacy and the State Department. The
extent to which our nation's priorities have been skewed
toward the military is illustrated by the resources we
invest in it compared to what we spend on diplomacy and
development. The base funding of the Department of
Defense is more than ten times that of the State Department and USAID.[6] Rather than a once-hoped-for "peace
dividend," our military planning remains predicated on
maintaining overwhelming superiority virtually everywhere on earth.

There are voices for change within the military
itself. One of the more comprehensive critiques comes
from Captain Wayne Porter, USN, and Colonel Mark
Mykleby, USMC, who want to adjust the balance between
exceptionalism and universalism toward the latter value,

still seeking to be "leader of the free world" but in a healthier and less military way. The officers' proposal for a new "National Strategic Narrative" calls for five shifts in approach:

1. From a dominant position of control to credible influence in a more open geopolitical system
2. From "containment to sustainment," based on domestic redevelopment and better modeling of the behavior we seek in other nations
3. From "deterrence and defense to civilian engagement and competition," which would reemphasize trade and diplomacy while still modernizing "a security complex that includes all domestic and foreign policy assets"
4. From "zero sum to positive sum global politics/ economics," preferring interdependence and universal values to isolation and exclusion of other nations
5. From "national security to national prosperity and security," a shift that would involve a new National Prosperity and Security Act to replace the 1947 National Security Act.[7]

Economic Drivers or National Purposes

President Eisenhower's prophetic warning about the unwarranted influence of the military-industrial complex in his 1961 farewell address has become more relevant than ever. More accurately called the military-industrial-congressional complex, or "the iron triangle," it is an interlocking system of mutually reinforcing interests with very little outside oversight. Supported by "political engineering" that distributes military contracts across many

From Eisenhower's Farewell Address, January 17, 1961

This conjunction of an immense military establishment and a large arms industry is new in the American experience. The total influence—economic, political, even spiritual—is felt in every city, every State house, every office of the Federal government. We recognize the imperative need for this development. Yet we must not fail to comprehend its grave implications. Our toil, resources, and livelihood are all involved; so is the very structure of our society.

In the councils of government, we must guard against the acquisition of unwarranted influence, whether sought or unsought, by the military-industrial complex. The potential for the disastrous rise of misplaced power exists and will persist.

We must never let the weight of this combination endanger our liberties or democratic processes. We should take nothing for granted. Only an alert and knowledgeable citizenry can compel the proper meshing of the huge industrial and military machinery of defense with our peaceful methods and goals, so that security and liberty may prosper together.

congressional districts, the complex creates and sustains its own bureaucratic momentum. How much are private interests dictating national interests, and have we come to confuse such interests with national purposes?

The United States' vast military and intelligence establishments go far beyond the intent or imagination of our nation's founders, whose views could loosely be called isolationist, opposed to "foreign entanglements," in John Adams's words. George Washington, in his farewell address, counseled against a significant standing army: "Overgrown military establishments are under any form of government inauspicious to liberty, and are to be regarded as particularly hostile to Republican liberty."[8] And James Madison wrote, "Of all enemies to public liberty, war is, perhaps, the most to be dreaded, because it comprises and develops the germ of every other. War is the parent of armies; from these proceed debts and taxes; and armies, and debts, and taxes are the known instruments for bringing the many under the domination of the few."[9]

Our founders were classically trained and thus knew how Rome itself had ceased to be a republic and had come to rule through co-opted local autocracies, how bread and circuses distracted the powerless, how conquest and slavery grew in economic importance, and how mercenaries replaced actual Romans in many of the legions. Richard Horsley and others have shown how the emperor cult was a form of binding civil religion that justified domination; Paul's assertion in chapter 13 of the letter to the Romans that God appoints governments, in fact, dismisses the claims of Roman gods and emperors and begins a process of accountability.[10]

By contrasting the practices of empire with "the highest ideals of our heritage," we affirm that our country should have a significant role in the world and one of benefit to all. It is a key role of the church to help inspire our culture to see new possibilities, and it is not isolationist to be opposed to much military intervention. At times the use of power is justified and may serve those high ideals of democracy and world community. The dangers are that our enormous arsenal calls to be used and that this mind-set may confuse power and responsibility. Finally, we note that when the United States goes on foreign adventures, as we did in Iraq—where we worked outside of international institutions and in violation of international laws that we helped create following World War II—we severely damage our moral legitimacy.[11] While some American nationalists would consider working through international institutions unrealistic and constraining, we call people to a deeper realism that recognizes the importance of moral legitimacy to international leadership. This lawful, cooperative, and moral approach is how we would characterize the "highest ideals of our heritage."

Challenges in Pulling the United States Back from Empire Practices

Professor Andrew Bacevich, a career military officer and now a professor of political science, analyzes a phenomenon he terms "Washington rules." These rules consist of the "American credo," which is the assumption that the United States is "indispensable"—that it alone has the duty and the calling to "lead, save, liberate, and ultimately transform the world."[12] This complements the belief in American exceptionalism. Both are consensus opinion across the spectrum of the American political elite, regardless of political party. This consensus insists that international peace and order require the United States to project military power anywhere across the globe and that the United States follow a policy of global interventionism. The twin pillars of "Washington rules"—American exceptionalism and the global police role—have a stranglehold on American foreign and military policy, according to Bacevich. Voices that question this consensus, as the church has done on numerous occasions, are regarded as outliers, too radical or too naïve and unrealistic. The result is a self-reinforcing system of decision making that discounts the calls for moral restraint or efforts to see the other nation's point of view.

Voices that question this consensus, as the church has done on numerous occasions, are regarded as outliers, too radical or too naïve and unrealistic. The result is a self-reinforcing system of decision making that discounts the calls for moral restraint or efforts to see the other nation's point of view.

Therefore, the church must be realistic about the nature of its influence. Three main factors influence military spending: (1) Powerful multinational corporations have a vested interest in perpetuating the machinery of war and seeing it as a necessity. Weapons must be used and new orders placed for profits to be maintained over time. (2) Political careers must be continued, and economic benefits from the military-industrial complex must continue to deliver the goods to constituencies back home, even if other forms of public investment would create more jobs. (3) The dramatic rise in the power of the Pentagon and the massive "defense" establishment over the past seventy years has created a huge and dominant sector of government with ever-increasing demands. These three extremely powerful factors in the decision-making process regarding war form a political "microclimate" largely impervious to outside influence and too often underestimated by churches and other reforming groups.

The Reformed tradition has long affirmed that the state can indeed be an instrument of God's purposes in history (Rom. 13). But the Word of God also warns us that the state can be an instrument of the Beast (Rev. 13). These texts pose the basic question of whether the United States functions more as an empire pursuing its own interests than as a faithful instrument of God's will. In these historical circumstances, nonviolence represents a counterlogic, a sharper contrast, and a counterweight to the machinery of permanent war and seemingly perpetual cycles of violence. The Reformed tradition makes careful provision for responsible resistance to government overreach, based on its covenantal vision of national purposes. This more constructive vision is the core of the alternatives to misused power that the church seeks to present. That covenantal vision was expressed in Puritan John Winthrop's first use of Jesus' metaphor of a "city set on a hill" for the new settlement they were building. Nowadays we are clearer than Winthrop was that human rights and respect for international law are essential building blocks in any such construction, but he was clear enough that for the community to last "we must be willing to abridge ourselves of our superfluities for the supply of others' necessities."[13]

Questions for Reflection

1. In your opinion, what is the peacemaking role of the church in the United States today?
2. Where have you seen the cross confused with the flag? Do you have a flag in your sanctuary? Has this ever been challenged?

3. How comfortable are you with naming the United States an empire. Does the shoe fit? Why or why not?

4. How should the church, as peacemaker, respond to the Washington rules? What would be our "Geneva rules"?

5. What does the church risk when it criticizes the government? Is the risk worth it in your opinion? Why or why not?

Risk Five, Part Two

Work for Peace

We commit ourselves to studying and practicing nonviolent means of conflict resolution, nonviolent methods for social change, and nonviolent opposition to war.

Part of Affirmation Four, as amended by the
222nd General Assembly (2016)*

Presbyterian Christians are looking for direction and guidance about how we can take faithful and effective action to reduce violence and war and to further justice and peace. There is broad interest in learning concrete peacemaking skills that we can use in our daily lives. Indeed, if we are to be effective peacemakers—able to actually reduce violence and injustice in our various contexts—then we need to receive education and training in the "'things that make for peace'" (Luke 19:42). To help bring about a more just and peaceful world, we

*Included in risk 5 is part of Affirmation Four of the peacemaking document "Risking Peace in a Violent World," approved by the 2016 General Assembly.

need to study and practice nonviolent means of conflict resolution (such as nonviolent communication, negotiation, and mediation) and nonviolent methods for social change, such as faith-based community organizing and nonviolent direct action. In this chapter we are specifically indebted to Rev. Roger Powers, consultant to the Peace Discernment process, who initially gathered some of the examples below. Powers is a pastor and former colleague of Gene Sharp, who has provided countless movements with a wide-range of nonviolent approaches.

This chapter is not only about nonviolent methods; the clear risk is that we try them *first* and understand them from the standpoint of principle and strategy. We also need to become more familiar with just-peacemaking initiatives, which can help prevent war, and just-war principles, which are intended to limit war. This will make us more effective advocates for justice and peace in the public square. Jesus' own statement "'If you . . . had only recognized on this day the things that make for peace!'" was addressed to the whole of Jerusalem and was followed shortly by his cleansing of the temple (Luke 19:42–46).

Besides the discussions of strategy, however, there is the question of whether the Reformed tradition itself should change to emphasize more the nonviolence of Jesus and to encourage nonviolent action when called to witness to sinful structures. Let us be clear that the rule of law endorsed in risk 2 does involve implicit coercion and that our complicity in structural violence makes any "pure" pacifism difficult (and un-Reformed!). Yet there is a significant difference between police and military approaches, and the former can be much more nonviolent than the latter. Certainly the sample of U.S. Presbyterians who engaged in the recent peace-discernment process generally felt that the fifteen years of war since

9/11 were counterproductive, deeply tragic, and literally demoralizing and wanted a shift in mind-set to proactive peacemaking, yet relatively few affirmed a thorough-going nonviolence. Recognizing that "you can't beat something with nothing," we focus here on changes in emphasis and method that may help reduce the level of violence in our statecraft and social relations. What follows is a kind of peacemaking toolbox; contact information and references are given in the resources section.

Interfaith Understanding

Among the most important peacemaking approaches for Christians today are practices of interreligious under-standing that build mutual respect and the ability to hear what is most important to the other, without vetoes or mischaracterization. Religions are often blamed for being the cause of conflict and violence in the world. Religious identity is impossible to separate from other dimensions of personal identity, yet those who blame religion isolate it as the primary causal factor. In reality, political, ethnic, and economic factors bear much more responsibility for creating the underlying conditions that lead to violent conflict. Nonetheless, religions have within them a storehouse of resources to promote peace and reconciliation, and Presbyterians should be quite familiar with the Christian basics, starting with the Golden Rule, "'Do to others as you would have them do to you'" (Luke 6:31), which is found in some form in all of the world's major religions. Public dialogue between religious leaders from opposing groups can help create breakthroughs for reconciliation.[1] Prophetic religious leaders are often among the few social actors who can and will take initiative in blocked situations.

Religions have within them a storehouse of
resources to promote peace and reconciliation,
and Presbyterians should be quite familiar with
the Christian basics, starting with the Golden
Rule, "'Do to others as you would have them
do to you'" (Luke 6:31), which is found in some
form in all of the world's major religions.

David Little, author of *Peacemaking in Action: Profiles of Religion in Conflict Resolution*, sees religious peacemakers playing four key roles: in "enforcement, peacekeeping, institution-and-capacity building, and agreement-making."[2] Though important for legitimacy, the religious role is less explicit in the first two of the four, enforcement, which can involve coercion to end violence (as in Bosnia and Kosovo), and peacekeeping, which can be diplomatic language for outside military monitoring or stabilization forces. The third and fourth roles, however, are sometimes considered part of a "track 2" or unofficial citizen diplomacy. They frequently involve religious peacemakers in the development of organizations and even rituals for social harmony, thus creating positive contexts for track 1, or formal peace negotiations. Such efforts built empathic understanding in South Sudan and Northern Ireland, for example, although the relationships built can remain fragile.

Nonviolent Communication and Conflict Resolution Skills

Too often the words we use, especially in conflictual situations, escalate tensions rather than reduce them. We use words as weapons to blame, judge, criticize, or dominate others. At the same time, we don't listen well. What we hear is distorted by our own prejudices and misconceptions. A specific form of nonviolent communication was developed by Marshall Rosenberg to help people exchange the information necessary to resolve conflicts and differences peacefully. When using nonviolent communication, people listen deeply to themselves and others and articulate their observations, feelings, needs, and requests honestly and respectfully with empathy and compassion. Nonviolent communication can help bring healing and reconciliation to interpersonal relationships in a variety of settings. More information is available from the Center for Nonviolent Communication (http://www.cnvc.org).

Conflict Resolution Skills

Methods of conflict resolution such as negotiation and mediation seek to settle disputes peacefully through mutual agreement. We encounter conflict regularly in our day-to-day lives—at home, at work, in school, and in our congregations. Knowing how to manage and resolve these conflicts well is essential to the well-being of ourselves and others. But few people ever receive training in conflict resolution.

Truth and Reconciliation Commissions

In risk 4 we noted ways that public forgiveness and apology were included within the just-peacemaking framework. Truth-and-reconciliation commissions are ways of bringing perpetrators of violence to acknowledge, if not actually confess, the truth of their actions before their victims or the survivors of their victims. The Rev. Allan Boesak, a leader of the nonviolent United Democratic Front that played a major role in South Africa's transition, has analyzed ambiguities in this quasi-judicial approach. The danger is that a collective evil, like apartheid, will be reduced to the actions of individuals who take the blame for a larger group that wants to minimize their shared complicity and "move on." Yet Boesak also affirms that victims can regain their voices and dignity through publicly recognized and respected grief.[3] The work of commissions must of course follow the actual achievement of cease-fires. The presence of outside observers (like Jimmy Carter) and religious leaders (like Desmond Tutu) can be extremely helpful. The key thing, though, is that such commissions are moral inventions, and they can lead to more healing and more creativity. We need more arenas where longer-term hostilities can be defused, young people inspired, and new leaders born.

In the areas of gun violence and mass incarceration in the United States, some churches and city police forces are teaming up to address structural violence with versions of these methods, inviting hostile gangs into neutral places, sharing stories of pain and redemption, and finding alternatives to punitive sentencing through more restorative and reparative justice.[4] And there are many veterans of foreign wars who can see the moral injuries carried by veterans of our domestic social conflicts.

Faith-Based Community Organizing and Other Grassroots Ecumenism

Congregations have joined together in faith-based community organizations to work for social and economic justice in their communities, as well as on matters such as crime and criminal justice as previously noted. By building relationships with one another, they discover their shared self-interest. By organizing their people and money, they build the power they need to influence key decision makers in government and business to act in the community's interests. Working across lines of religion, race, and class, these interfaith community organizations have fought for affordable housing, better schools, funding for social services, and a host of other issues. These are efforts that address causes of structural violence and hence contribute to the decrease of violence in families and communities.

In terms of ecumenical resources, not all, of course, need to come from the grass roots to help local and regional efforts. The Social Creed for the 21st Century, adopted unanimously by the National Council of Churches' Governing Board in late 2007 (as well as by the Presbyterian General Assembly in 2008), forged a remarkable one-page consensus about what the churches stand for in public life—with agreement from the historic black churches and the Orthodox churches, as well as the "mainline" Protestants. It provides a Trinitarian framework and has three goals particularly related to this study:

- Peacemaking through multilateral diplomacy rather than unilateral force, the abolition of torture, and a strengthening of the United Nations and the rule of international law.
- Nuclear disarmament and redirection of military spending to more peaceful and productive uses.
- Cooperation and dialogue for peace and environmental justice among the world's religions.[5]

Accompaniment and Nonviolent
Third-Party Intervention

Nonviolent direct action is usually initiated by the "weaker" party in a conflict. In recent decades, however, there has been growing experience with third parties, who are not part of a conflict, intervening nonviolently in the hopes of deterring violent attacks and human rights violations. The Presbyterian Church (U.S.A.) has played a part in these efforts through its support for Witness for Peace, a body that brought accompaniers to Nicaragua during the Contra War against the Sandinista government of Nicaragua, from 1983 to 1990. Since 2005, the Colombia Accompaniment Program, started by the Presbyterian Peace Fellowship with support from the Presbyterian Peacemaking Program, has brought over ninety trained accompaniers to stand in solidarity with the Iglesia Presbiteriana de Colombia, which had lost leaders to death squads and whose members had been intimidated for resisting land grabs by the powerful. The World Council of Churches has cosponsored an accompaniment program in Palestine to protect Palestinian school children and others from settler and Israeli army violence. The goal in such efforts is "to see and be seen." At a less-intense level, court watchers and election monitors do variants of this work.

There is perhaps some divine irony in the use of U.S. citizenship—so often the mark of "First World" privilege—as the means for protecting citizens of other countries from their own governments—especially if those governments want to receive U.S. military subsidies and perhaps protection from censure in the United Nations. Such observers need considerable training and great moral resolve to be able to endure the resentment and harassment they receive from brutal settlers, unjust officials, or corrupt police. Yet if we remember the four U.S. Roman Catholic churchwomen who were brutalized and killed in El Salvador by a government strongly supported by the Reagan administration, we know that those martyred women "saved" an unknown number of Salvadorans from those same off-duty military death squads.

Teaching Peace in the Church

The more personal dimensions and disciplines of active nonviolence and peacemaking are already being practiced in many churches: strangers are welcomed; refugees are resettled; prisoners are visited; veterans are brought in; "international peacemakers" are hosted; and interfaith dialogues are sponsored. Some mission trips also seek to cross once-hostile boundaries or to help build new friendships. Suspicion of "the Russians" still exists; racism still poisons our nation; and Islamophobia is manipulated to prevent empathic understanding: all are addressed in some congregations. Some churches also teach children nonviolence and ways to prevent bullying. Increasing numbers are speaking up about the constant menace of gun violence. We believe these life-giving practices are of God and offer life to the church and witness to the world.

Peacemaking is a faith commitment; it is a calling rather than a conclusion. It constitutes the lens by which reality is brought into focus and is the value system by which the meaning and significance of threats are determined. With humility, we recognize that just as the nationalistic exceptionalism of empire distorts, so a concern for universal human rights may not be the full key to the healing of the nations. If the United States were to reduce its footprint, would benign forces take the place of our military?

Would the churches push for constructive multilateral ways to fill power vacuums and help create order through collective security—or are we simply weary of war? We have spoken of citizen diplomacy; could we see ourselves assisting others with citizen-based defense? At the core of all these risks in seeking peace is the choice to resist violence, and it is not just a personal choice.

> Peacemaking is a faith commitment; it
> is a calling rather than a conclusion.

Three Examples of Risking Peace

The verb "making" implied in Matthew 5:9's "'Blessed are the peacemakers'" is *poesis* in Greek. Peacemaking is thus a creative and even poetic work. The gospel of peace is Christ, who is our peace, who gives to us ministries of reconciliation, who makes us ambassadors of God's commonwealth and reign. But perhaps God also calls us to be poets of peace—composers, crafters, creators, hearers, and doers of peace.[6] Let us look at three true stories, each of which shows a different range of personal or group courage and moral imagination.

Le Chambon

The French village of Le Chambon risked peace in sheltering 5,000 Jews fleeing the Nazis during World War II. The driving force behind the rescue effort was Andre Trocme, the Huguenot (French Reformed) pastor of the village. Deeply committed to Christian nonviolence, on Sunday mornings he would preach the Sermon on the Mount, love of God and love of neighbor, reverence for life, and the necessity of resisting evil with good. The people of Le Chambon hid Jews in their homes and farm-houses and arranged for them to reach the safe haven of neutral Switzerland. In doing so, they risked their lives. Occasionally, the Gestapo raided the town. Leaders were arrested and imprisoned, and some were later killed. But despite the repression, the resistance in Le Chambon continued to the end of the war.

In the last months of German occupation, the Tartar Legion commanded by SS Colonel Metzger was poised to destroy the village and its inhabitants. But a second German officer, Major Schmehling, commandant of the German army post in Le Puy, dissuaded Metzger from attacking. Years after the war, Schmehling told Trocme of the fateful conversation: "Colonel Metzger was a hard one, and he kept insisting that we move in on Le Chambon. But I kept telling him to wait. . . . I told Metzger that this kind of resistance has nothing to do with violence, nothing to do with anything we could destroy with violence. With all my personal and military power I opposed sending his legion into Le Chambon."[7]

From today's vantage point, more than seventy years after these events, two points may be added to this still-gripping story. The author of the book *Lest Innocent Blood Be Shed*, Philip Hallie, was a philosopher of Jewish background. His life quest was for examples of human goodness, and another of his books, *In the Eye of the Hurricane*, provides a number of other examples. Risk-taking leadership is key in them, but so are dedicated, often Christian communities that sustain the individual members. A second point would be that Protestants in France then and now are a tiny minority. Yet they used their difference to hold themselves to a very high standard and to resist the culture around them.

Ronald E. McNair Discovery Learning Academy near Atlanta

More recently, on August 20, 2013, a school bookkeeper, Antoinette Tuff, risked peace when a gunman walked into her school. Twenty-year-old Michael Brandon Hill entered the Ronald E. McNair Discovery Learning Academy near Atlanta with an AK-47 and five hundred rounds of ammunition, intending to shoot and kill as many people as he could. Ms. Tuff was scared but remained calm. She had received training in how to respond to dangerous situations like this one. And she found courage and strength in her Christian faith. She recalled her pastor's teachings about "anchoring and how you anchor yourself in the Lord." She was able to talk Hill down and convince him to surrender to police, thereby averting another mass shooting. "It was all God," she said. "I was just praying."[8]

Particularly in light of the killing of eleven African American Bible-study participants by a young white racist at Mother Emanuel Church in Charleston, South Carolina, the possibility of defusing a situation like Ms. Tuff did must be held out—even if the United States is marked by a shooting of three or more people *at once* virtually every day. The availability of guns and perhaps the spread of nihilism and self-destruction as much as hate fuels these grimly repetitive episodes, far more dangerous than our acts of explicit domestic terrorism, which are themselves more frequent than terrorism by the foreign born. We should celebrate Ms. Tuff for keeping her head and her praying heart in a truly dangerous situation, but our culture also needs to keep its head and heart in racheting down fear into realistic ways of disarming the dangerous in our culture rather than enflaming them. Racism and resentment are parts of this story; the church as truth teller needs to help detoxify the currents of rage, but we must also be prepared to demonstrate and to mourn publicly when senseless and preventable tragedies occur.

Chemical Weapons in Syria, 2013

The United States risked peace in September 2013 when it opted not to launch air strikes against Syria in response to an August 21 chemical weapons attack against civilians, but instead negotiated an international agreement to disarm the Syrian government of its chemical weapons. President Obama threatened a military response as a consequence for violating international norms. Military intervention seemed imminent. Then U.S. Secretary of State John Kerry made an off-the-cuff remark that air strikes could be averted if Syria turned over all its chemical weapons to the international community, but Syria "isn't about to do it, and it can't be done."[9] This rhetorical suggestion was taken up as a serious proposal by Russia and received a positive response from Syria. Where once military intervention was being touted as the only option for responding to the use of chemical weapons in Syria, the United States stumbled into a diplomatic alternative that had not been seriously considered. It is another question whether the countries involved in that grinding proxy war—including the United States and Russia more directly—have yet begun a serious peace process as of late 2016, despite waves of desperate refugees that have destabilized Europe.

Clearly there was a virtue in having an administration that could "walk back" from a red line rather than be bound by pride or the need to show "credibility." In fact, the U.S. government and others seems to have underestimated the strength of the religious cohesion of the Syrian Alawite community of which President Assad is a part.

The tragedy of Syria deserves more analysis than we provide here or earlier in risk 4. Nonviolent Christian groups in Syria continue to provide food, shelter, and schooling, trying to break down suspicion among the various ethnic and religious groups, praying and preparing for a lasting cease-fire and even return of the displaced millions. Yet the lessons have to include the need for a world order that is stronger even than the strongest nations, which continue to allow weapons sales and covert strategies to prolong a dreadful proxy war full of countless war crimes and human rights violations.

Summary

God is always doing a new thing. It is the nature of God to gather up all the occasions of the past and, with immense healing power, weave transforming possibilities into the emerging moment. The future is constantly arriving, a future whose radical and redemptive newness it owes to the creative work of the Poet of the World, the Lover of Souls, the Lord of the Church, who declares, "'See, I am making all things new'" (Rev. 21:5). Let us welcome the new thing that God is doing, risk peace and transform conflict by boldly practicing the things that make for peace.

Peacemaking Charge

The 2016 General Assembly finally adopted as its fifth affirmation the following doxology-like charge:

> We place our faith, hope, and trust in God alone.
> We renounce violence as a means to further selfish
> national interests, to procure wealth, or to dominate

others. We will practice boldly the things that make for peace and look for the day when "they shall beat their swords into ploughshares, and their spears into pruning-hooks; nation shall not lift up sword against nation, neither shall they learn war anymore.

Questions for Reflection

1. How have you worked for peace in the past? What do you think is most important in working for peace today?
2. What risks will this involve for you? For the church?
3. Which example of risking peace inspired you the most? Why?
4. Thinking back on the five risks for peacemaking, which stands out the most in your mind? Why?
5. Which is most urgent for the church to address? Why?
6. What actions will you take as a result of these five risks?

Afterword

The five risks adopted by the 2016 Presbyterian General Assembly described in this book were confirmed a few months prior to the divisive 2016 U.S. general election. The new administration is more nationalist and has questioned international alliances, trade, and foreign assistance while emphasizing military strength and increased military spending. The risks Christian peacemakers must take become even riskier and more urgent in a time like this. Let's take a moment and look at each risk and what some implications might be in this time.

The first risk of peacemaking is to present nonviolent alternatives, ways of resisting the pull of war and the misuse of power. Christian discipleship has a prophetic component that should continue to be exercised in public witness and grounded in prayer, communal worship, personal giving, and practices of compassion. The church speaks to policies, not personalities or parties, and needs to find new ways for its voice to be heard. And sometimes this needs to take the form of protest.

In the 2016 election process, we did not hear much about the morality of war, and faith got token attention. Without a sense of God's gracious sovereignty, the love of country in patriotism can become the idolatry of nationalism. In such a climate, people can be more easily demonized and denied their rights, silenced, and even tortured. So the risk for peacemakers is higher when they advocate for reconciliation "even at risk to national security," as the Confession of 1967 forthrightly states. On a basic level, the use of force by police and military can be encouraged for authoritarian purposes when a nation or leader is elevated too high. Let us remember that "peace is patriotic" and that truth is the first casualty in wars—and in tyrannies.

Was the election rigged against love of neighbor? To the extent that polarization is encouraged by our long, marketing-driven campaigns, then personal attacks, hacking, distracting allegations, and making voting hard for people are accepted by many as part of what your side or team "has to do to win." We understand external interference in other countries' elections, but we were supposed to be an exception. Beyond the dysfunctions of our system, however, there is a need for peacemaking in U.S. politics itself.

The second risk is to face our complicity in social as well as personal sin, and thus risk 2 looks at the structural evils of racism, sexism, and economic injustice. It gives particular attention to our shared complicity in the conduct of the Iraq, Afghan, and other interventions. In the election, fear of Muslims, terrorism, and immigrants generally was amplified, and we debated how much to distrust China or trust Russia. Explicitly evangelical candidates lost in the primary process, but even self-proclaimed evangelicals seemed to subordinate Christianity to Americanism, and given the undercurrents of racism seen at campaign rallies, that Americanism was sometimes assumed to be nonimmigrant whiteness. At the same time, there were forms of idealism and hope across the political spectrum, and a Democratic Socialist primary candidate received unprecedented support. Thus despite our entanglements in the grid of systemic injustice, peacemakers can still risk calling on the ideals and hopes that God inspires in all people, including those in politics and the military.

Where the second risk gets tougher is in resisting the politics of resentment. Beyond the loss of civility in public life, there is a loss of the kind of "civil religion" that sought unity and a sense of covenant with all citizens. While civil religion can compromise the church when it idealizes history, the idea of a national covenant also carries high ideals and was influenced by Reformed theology. Citizenship gains purpose when freedoms require responsibilities, the strong take care of the weak, and it is a matter of self-respect for everybody to pay taxes and obey laws. We lose such a national covenant when we scorn undesirable groups, abandon the poor, and put military burdens disproportionately on the economically disadvantaged.

The third risk asks us to reclaim Jesus of Nazareth as the Prince of Peace—to be willing to look at what the last twenty years of scholarship say about Jesus' own nonviolent movement. The urgency of today's dangers adds the risk of moving too quickly to ethics and strategy. Peacemaking in risk 3 is about God's redemptive work in the world, which we sum up in the word "Christ." The pattern of Christ, according to Luke Timothy Johnson, is not speculation but the basic path of a moral leader who gives his or her life for others. Salvation for us is anchored in moral perceptions and involves descent as well as ascent, dying and rising, suffering and forgiving and finding our "true" selves transformed. It is about "the power of love rather than the love of power," not about personal bliss but about justice for human communities. It involves a different kind of kingship or rule, grows from the death-dealing cross, and outgrows all competitions for glory. The early Christians saw in Jesus of Nazareth the suffering servant of Isaiah and heard from him equally prophetic words of judgment and grace.

So we're clear: peacemaking has a theological reality that is tested in all our relationships, from small to large. It is also a discipline of faith that requires "moral imagination," in that complex social conflicts make ethical principles hard to apply. We need to be formed and sustained by congregations with strong internal cultures that reflect God's integrity and purpose for all creation. Our grounding in the Christian tradition may then give us insight into serious moral work and spiritual experience in other traditions. The pattern of Christ for us reveals universal truth. Thus we can see not only the divine image—which is good as Genesis says—but the face of Christ in people's prophetic courage everywhere in this world. Interfaith peacemaking carries its own risks but can be a deeply Christian enterprise.

The fourth risk is learning to use the methods of non-violence and the strategic approaches of just peacemaking. The years ahead will be full of tests of conscience on a very large scale, shaking political leaders and political structures. There will be "wars and rumors of wars," bad news and false news, deliberate spiritual hacking of trust and other forms of betrayal. The temptations to oversimplify, to seek pseudosaviors and strongmen, and to lash out in vengeance will all rush in if our spiritual houses are empty. And tribalism will lock out the claims and cries of others.

We must be the "honest patriots" (in Donald Shriver's phrase) who can admit and correct our nation's mistakes. It means the risks of modeling the humility necessary for truthfulness. Presbyterians and many other Christians were crucial in pushing for the Universal Declaration of Human Rights and organizations like the United Nations based on international law. Their twentieth-century creations have obvious defects, but they were right that institutions as well as leaders are needed and that true leaders need to see beyond barriers of nation, class, gender, and other divisions. (They even need to see far ahead, to that seventh generation.)

The fifth risk is to convert the empire, which also means preventing the rise of emperors. In that two-chapter challenge we stuck with the biblical language of empire, which the earlier wording contrasted with the "highest ideals of our tradition." Those ideals seek the best for others as well as ourselves, a language of moral diplomacy. As the church continues its witness, "in season and out of season," our biggest common threat is that the weather itself is becoming "out of season." As a result, millions of angry and desperate climate refugees will be seeking higher or more fertile ground as seas rise and deserts spread. Perhaps political mood swings in the U.S. electorate are a bit like increasingly erratic weather patterns, but the people seeking to escape climate change will be real. Other nations will also intensify the drive to control resources.

Psalm 146 tells us not to put our trust in princes (or princesses), but that lesson may be applied to any single nation trying to go it alone, however populist the fantasy may be. Global warming is real science, not science fiction, though sci fi often imagines the crash of civilizations and dreams of new saviors with new technological powers. The Savior we already have, however, helps teach us the proven social technology of peacemaking. What we have also been given, by the power of the Spirit, is the ability to imagine and work for a community of peoples who make peace among themselves so as to make peace with a groaning creation.

So it comes back to taking risks for peace, based in our faith experience of the possibility of reconciliation. The five risks in this book give us grounding and strategy. All we need to do is take action.

Resources

Interreligious Peace Building

Training and educational resources are available from a number of organizations:

- The Tanenbaum Center for Interreligious Understanding (https://www.tanenbaum.org)
- The Berkley Center for Religion, Peace & World Affairs (http://berkleycenter.georgetown.edu)
- The Religion and Peacemaking Program of the U.S. Institute of Peace (https://www.usip.org /issue-areas/religion)
- The Program on Religion and Reconciliation at the Kroc Institute for International Peace Studies (http://kroc.nd.edu/)
- Council for a Parliament of the World's Religions (https://berkleycenter.georgetown.edu/organiza tions/council-for-a-parliament-of-the-world-s -religions)
- Religions for Peace (http://www.religionsfor peace.org)

Conflict Resolution Skills

Many community mediation centers offer training in conflict resolution skills. For church leaders who want to learn the skills needed to address conflict in church settings, the Lombard Mennonite Peace Center (http://www.lmpeacecenter.org) offers a Mediation Skills Training Institute for Church Leaders. Excellent educational resources are also available through the Program on Negotiation at Harvard Law School (http://www.pon.harvard.edu).

Faith-Based Community Organizing

Training in faith-based community organizing is available through four national organizing networks. We also note an example of a local organizing group focused on gun violence:

- The Industrial Areas Foundation (http://www.industrialareasfoundation.org)
- The Gamaliel Foundation (www.gamaliel.org)
- The PICO National Network (http://www.piconetwork.org)
- The Direct Action and Research Training Center (DART) (http://www.thedartcenter.org/)
- Heeding God's Call (http://heedinggodscall.org/)

Nonviolent Third-Party Intervention

Most nonviolent direct action has been used by one or more parties directly engaged in a conflict. However, in the past few decades there has been growing experience with third parties, who are not part of a conflict, intervening nonviolently in the hopes of deterring violent attacks and human rights violations. Several organizations recruit, train, and deploy volunteers who provide an international nonviolent presence in areas of violent conflict. They include:

- Peace Brigades International (http://www.peace brigades.org/)
- Witness for Peace (http://www.witnessforpeace .org/)
- Christian Peacemaker Teams (http://www.cpt .org/)
- Nonviolent Peaceforce (http://www.nonviolent peaceforce.org/)
- Ecumenical Accompaniment Programme in Palestine and Israel (http://www.eappi.org/)

Notes

Risk One: Commit to the Gospel of Peace

1. Edward L. Long, "The Mandate to Seek a Just Peace," in *The Peacemaking Struggle: Militarism & Resistance*, ed. Ronald H. Stone and Dana Wilbanks (Lanham, MD: University Press of America, 1985), 29–41.
2. "Resources for Study of Christian Obedience in a Nuclear Age" (Office of the General Assembly, 1988).
3. Donald E. Gowan and Ulrich W. Mauser, "Shalom and Eirene," in Stone and Wilbanks, *The Peacemaking Struggle*, 132–33.

Risk Two: Confessing Our Complicity

1. *The Constitution of the Presbyterian Church (U.S.A.)*, Part I, *Book of Confessions* (Louisville, KY: Office of the General Assembly, Presbyterian Church (U.S.A.), 2016), 11.4, line 69.
2. "Firearm Homicides and Suicides in Major Metropolitan Areas—United States, 2006–2007 and 2009–2010," Centers for Disease Control and Prevention, August 2, 2013, https://www.cdc.gov /mmwr/preview/mmwrhtml/mm6230a1.htm.
3. Michele C. Black et al., *The National Intimate Partner and Sexual Violence Survey: 2010 Summary Report*, Center for Injury Prevention and Control (November 2011): 2, https://www.cdc.gov/violence prevention/pdf/nisvs_executive_summary-a.pdf.

4. Mark Douglas, "Violence," in *Dictionary of Scripture and Ethics*, ed. Joel Green (Grand Rapids: Baker Academic, 2011), 809.

5. "Child Poverty," National Center for Children in Poverty, http://nccp.org/topics/childpoverty.html. The University of Michigan's Gerald Ford Center also corroborates this data, placing the number of children in poverty at 21.1 percent in 2014. See http://www.npc.umich.edu/poverty/.

6. Justin Wolfers, "The Gains from the Economic Recovery Are Still Limited to the Top One Percent," http://www.nytimes.com/2015/01/28/upshot/gains-from-economic-recovery-still-limited-to-top-one-percent.html; and Josh Bivens, "The Top 1 Percent's Share of Income from Wealth Has Been Rising for Decades," http://www.epi.org/publication/top-1-percents-share-income-wealth-rising/.

7. Walter Wink, "The Myth of Redemptive Violence," http://www2.goshen.edu/~joannab/women/wink99.pdf.

8. Martin Luther King Jr., *Where Do We Go from Here: Chaos or Community* (Boston: Beacon Press, 2010; original publication, 1967), 62.

9. Christian Parenti, *Tropic of Chaos: Climate Change and the New Geography of Violence* (New York: Nation Books, 2011).

10. Isabel Ortiz and Matthew Cummins, "Global Inequality: Beyond the Bottom Billion," UNICEF Social and Economic Policy Working Paper, April 2011, 12, http://www.unicef.org/socialpolicy/files/Global_Inequality.pdf.

11. George Kennan, "Review of Current Trends, U.S. Foreign Policy, Policy Planning Staff, PPS No. 23. Top Secret," in *Foreign Relations of the United States, 1948*, vol. 1, pt. 2, U.S. Department of State (Washington D.C. Government Printing Office, 1976), 524–25, http://digicoll.library.wisc.edu/cgi-bin/FRUS/FRUS-idx?typ=goto&id=FRUS.FRUS1948v01p2&isize=M&submit=Go+to+page&page=524.

12. Thomas L. Friedman, "A Manifesto for the Fast World," *New York Times*, March 28, 1999, http://www.nytimes.com/1999/03/28/magazine/a-manifesto-for-the-fast-world.html

13. Watson Institute, Brown University, "Costs of War," http://watson.brown.edu/costsofwar/costs/human/civilians.

14. UNHRC, "Global Forced Displacement Hits Record High," http://www.unhcr.org/en-us/news/latest/2016/6/5763b65a4/global-forced-displacement-hits-record-high.html.

15. For Department of Defense data by recent war, see https://www.defense.gov/casualty.pdf.

16. "Costs of War," Watson Institute for International and Public Affairs, Brown University, updated September 2016, http://watson.brown.edu/costsofwar/costs/economic. "The Costs of War project is a team of thirty-five scholars, legal experts, human rights practitioners, and physicians that began its work in 2011." The project is based at the Watson Institute of Brown University, Providence, Rhode Island.

17. Ben Farmer, "Wars in Iraq and Afghanistan were a 'failure' costing £29bn," The Telegraph, May 8, 2014, http://www.telegraph.co.uk/news/uknews/defence/10859545/Wars-in-Iraq-and-Afghanistan-were-a-failure-costing-29bn.html.

18. See Catherine Lutz and Sujaya Desai, "US Reconstruction Aid for Afghanistan: The Dollars and Sense," January 5, 2015, Watson Institute for International Studies, Brown University, http://watson.brown.edu/costsofwar/files/cow/imce/papers/2015/US%20Reconstruction%20Aid%20for%20Afghanistan.pdf.

19. The cost comparisons in this section are distilled from "U.S. Security Spending Since 9/11," May 16, 2011, National Priorities Project, http://nationalpriorities.org/analysis/2011/us-security-spending-since-911/. Also see David Cecere, "New Study Finds 45,000 Deaths Annually Linked to Lack of Health Coverage," *Harvard Gazette*, September 17, 2009, http://news.harvard.edu/gazette/story/2009/09/new-study-finds-45000-deaths-annually-linked-to-lack-of-health-coverage/.

Risk Three: Reclaim Christ the Peacemaker

1. Luke Timothy Johnson, *The Real Jesus: The Misguided Quest for the Historical Jesus and the Truth of the Traditional Gospels* (San Francisco: Harper Collins, 1996), 149.

2. Richard B. Hays, *The Moral Vision of the New Testament: Community, Cross, New Creation, A Contemporary Introduction to New Testament Ethics* (New York: Harper Collins, 1996), 329.

3. Ibid., 331–32.

4. Richard A. Horsley, *Jesus and the Spiral of Violence: Popular Jewish Resistance in Roman Palestine* (Minneapolis: Fortress Press, 1993), 319.

5. Andrea Bartoli, keynote presentation, Montreat College Peace Discernment Conference, January 21, 2014 (transcript available from ACSWP).

6. Martin Luther King Jr., *Strength to Love* (Philadelphia: Fortress Press, 1981), 39.

7. Johnson, *The Real Jesus*, 149.

8. Ronald H. Stone, "The Justifiable War Tradition," in *The Peacemaking Struggle: Militarism & Resistance*, ed. Ronald H. Stone and Dana Wilbanks(Lanham, MD: University Press of America, 1985), 187.

9. Albert Curry Winn, *Ain't Gonna Study War No More* (Louisville, KY: Westminster/John Knox Press, 1993), 99, cited in Daniel J. Ott, "Toward a Realistic, Public, Christian Pacifism" *American Journal of Theology & Philosophy* 33, no. 3 (September 2012): 245–57.

10. Jerome F. D. Creach, *Violence in Scripture* (Louisville, KY: Westminster/John Knox Press, 2013).

11. Ott, "Toward a Realistic, Public, Christian Pacifism," 254.

12. This paragraph is from the Reverends Mark Davidson and Roger Powers, both pastors on the Peace Discernment Steering Team, putting recent scholarship into admittedly simplified antitheses. Davidson is pastor of Church of Reconciliation, Chapel Hill, North Carolina, and Powers is pastor of St. Andrew Presbyterian Church, Albuquerque, New Mexico. See https://www.pc-biz.org/#/committee/575/business, third section of "Risking Peace in a Violent World."

13. Victor Paul Furnish, "Uncommon Love and the Common Good: Christians as Citizens in the Letters of Paul," in *In Search of the Common Good*, ed. Patrick D. Miller and Dennis P. McCann (New York/London: T. & T. Clark, 2005).

14. These phrases come from Stanley Hauerwas and William H. Willimon, *Resident Aliens: Life in the Christian Colony* (Nashville: Abingdon, 1989) and reflect Furnish's biblical argument for a more Reformed and Catholic reading of Paul.

Risk Four: Practice New Peace Strategies

1. Maria Stephan and Erica Chenoweth, "Why Civil Resistance Works: The Strategic Logic of Nonviolent Conflict," *International Security* 33, no.1 (Summer 2008): 7–44, http://www.mitpress journals.org/doi/pdf/10.1162/isec.2008.33.1.7.

2. Ibid.

3. Kermit D. Johnson, "Just War and Nuclear Deterrence," in *The Peacemaking Struggle: Militarism & Resistance*, ed. Ronald H. Stone

and Dana W. Wilbanks (Lanham, MD: University Press of America, 1985), 197.

4. Ibid., 192.

5. Ibid.

6. Quoted in David S., "The Nuclear Freeze," Presbyterian Historical Society, September 9, 2014, http://www.history.pcusa.org/blog/2014/09/nuclear-freeze.

7. Chris Hedges, *War Is a Force That Gives Us Meaning* (New York: PublicAffairs, 2002).

8. Leonel Narvaez, *Political Culture of Forgiveness and Reconciliation* (Bogotá: Fundación Para La Reconcilión, 2009 [original Spanish] and 2010 [English].) Includes essays by Narvaez and Hicks.

9. Mel Baars O'Malley, "War and the Dimensions of Love," Faith and Leadership, September 10, 2012, http://www.faithandleadership.com/content/mel-baars-war-and-the-dimensions-love.

10. Rita Nakashima-Brock and Gabriella Lettini, *Soul Repair: Recovery from Moral Injury after War* (Boston: Beacon Press, 2012).

11. John Paul Lederach, *The Moral Imagination: The Art and Soul of Building Peace* (Oxford: Oxford University Press, 2005), 14

Risk Five, Part One: To Convert the Empire (Again!)

1. Scott Stern, Amy Wares, and Tamar Hellman, *Social Progress Index 2016 Methodological Report*, July 1, 2016, http://www.socialprogressimperative.org/publication/2016-social-progress-index-methodological-report/.

2. Accra Declaration, para. 10, https://www.presbyterianmission.org/resource/accra-confession-covenant-justice-economy-and-eart/.

3. Fandos, Nicholas, "U.S. Foreign Arms Deals Increased Nearly $10 Billion in 2014," *The New York Times*, December 25, 2015, http://www.nytimes.com/2015/12/26/world/middleeast/us-foreign-arms-deals-increased-nearly-10-billion-in-2014.html.

4. Angelo Young, "Global Defense Budget Seen Climbing In 2014," February 6, 2014, http://www.ibtimes.com/global-defense-budget-seen-climbing-2014-first-total-increase-2009-russia-surpasses-britain-saudi.

5. Dana Priest and William M. Arkin, "A Hidden World, Growing beyond Control," last updated September, 2010, http://projects.washingtonpost.com/top-secret-america/articles/a-hidden-world-growing-beyond-control/.

6. Kimberly Amadeo, "U.S. Military Budget: Components, Challenges, Growth," *The Balance* (blog), https://www.thebalance.com/u-s-military-budget-components-challenges-growth-3306320.

7. Anne-Marie Slaughter, preface to "A National Strategic Narrative," http://www.scifun.org/Readings/A_National_Strategic_Narrative.pdf.

8. George Washington, "Washington's Farewell Address 1796," Yale Law School, http://avalon.law.yale.edu/18th_century/washing.asp.

9. James Madison, "Political Observations, 20 April 1795," Founders Online, https://founders.archives.gov/documents/Madison/01-15-02-0423.

10. See Robert Jewett, "Response: Exegetical Support from Romans and other Letters," in *Paul and Politics*, ed. Richard Horsley (Harrisburg, PA: Trinity Press International, 2000), 67.

11. John Ikenberry, *Liberal Leviathan: The Origins, Crisis and Transformation of the American World Order* (Princeton, NJ: Princeton University Press, 2012).

12. Andrew J. Bacevich, *Washington Rules: America's Path to Permanent War* (New York: Metropolitan/Macmillan, 2010), 12; following pages describe the credo's history.

13. John Winthrop, "A Model of Christian Charity," accessed on December 15, 2016, http://www.goodreads.com/author/quotes/519465.John_Winthrop.

Risk Five, Part Two: Work for Peace

1. David Little, ed., *Peacemakers in Action: Profiles of Religion in Conflict Resolution* (New York: Cambridge University Press/Tanenbaum Center for Interreligious Understanding, 2007).

2. Ibid., 442–47.

3. Allan Boesak included this analysis in his presentation to the Consultation on Peace Discernment for Presbyterian-related colleges and universities, January 19, 2013.

4. Some of these approaches are described in the 2010 General Assembly policy *Gun Violence, Gospel Values*, https://www.pcusa.org/site_media/media/uploads/acswp/pdf/gun-violence-policy.pdf.

5. *Connecting to the Creed* 9. The booklet also contains handy preaching references for each goal of the Social Creed, itself modeled on the pioneering 1908 Social Creed of the Churches, http://www.presbyterianmission.org/ministries/compassion-peace-justice/acswp/social-creed/.

6. Andrea Bartoli suggested this understanding of peacemaking as an art in his keynote at the Consultation on Peace Discernment for Presbyterian-related colleges and universities, January 19, 2013.

7. Philip Hallie, *Lest Innocent Blood Be Shed: The Story of the Village of Le Chambon and How Goodness Happened There* (New York: Harper & Row, 1979), 245.

8. Lee Woofenden, "Antoinette Tuff and the Averted School Shooting: God's Love in Action," Spiritual Insights for Everyday Life, August 28, 2013, https://leewoof.org/2013/08/28/antoinette-tuff -and-the-averted-school-shooting-gods-love-in-action/.

9. Michael R. Gordon and Steven Lee Myers, "Obama Calls Russia Offer on Syria Possible 'Breakthrough'" *New York Times*, September 9, 2013, http://www.nytimes.com/2013/09/10/world/middle east/kerry-says-syria-should-hand-over-all-chemical-arms.html?page wanted=all&_r=0.

Further Reading

On Dimensions of Peacemaking Strategy

Hauerwas, Stanley. *War and the American Difference: Theological Reflections on Violence and National Identity*. Grand Rapids: Baker Academic, 2013.

Horsley, Richard A. *Jesus and the Powers: Conflict, Covenant, and the Hope of the Poor*. Minneapolis: Fortress Press, 2011.

King, Martin Luther Jr. *I Have A Dream: Writings and Speeches that Changed the World*. Edited by James M. Washington. San Francisco: HarperCollins, 1992.

Lederach, John Paul. *The Journey Toward Reconciliation*. Scottsdale, PA: Herald Press, 1999.

Little, David, ed. *Peacemakers in Action: Profiles of Religion in Conflict Resolution*. New York: Cambridge University Press/Tanenbaum Center for Interreligious Understanding, 2007.

Nakashima-Brock, Rita, and Gabriella Lettini. *Soul Repair: Recovery from Moral Injury After War*. Boston: Beacon Press, 2012.

Sharp, Gene. *From Dictatorship to Democracy: A Conceptual Framework for Liberation*. New York: New Press, 2002; reprint, 2012.

Stassen, Glen, ed. *Just Peacemaking: Ten Practices for Abolishing War*. Cleveland: Pilgrim Press, 1998.

Ufford-Chase, Rick. *Faithful Resistance: Gospel Visions for the Church in a Time of Empire*. UNCO.org/Unshelved, 2016.

Wink, Walter, ed. *Peace is the Way: Writings on Nonviolence from the Fellowship of Reconciliation*. Maryknoll, NY: Orbis, 2000.

Theological and Ethical Discussion of War and Peace Issues

Avram, Wes, ed. *Anxious about Empire: Theological Essays on the New Global Realities*. Grand Rapids: Brazos Press, 2004.

Hedges, Chris. *War Is a Force That Gives Us Meaning*. New York: PublicAffairs, 2002.

Iosso, Christian. "The Church Reformed, Always Resisting," in *Applied Christian Ethics*. Edited by Matthew Lon Weaver. Lanham, MD: Lexington Books, 2014.

Long, Edward Leroy, Jr. *Facing Terrorism: Responding as Christians*. Louisville, KY: Westminster/John Knox Press, 2004.

Love, Greg Anderson. *Love, Violence, and the Cross: How the Nonviolent God Saves Us through the Cross of Christ*. Eugene, OR: Cascade Books, 2010.

Lunger, Harold L., ed. *Facing War, Waging Peace: Findings of the American Church Study Conferences, 1940–60*. New York: Friendship Press, 1988.

Raynal, Charles E. "The Response of American Protestantism to World War II and Atomic Weapons." In *Peace, War and God's Justice*. Edited by Thomas D. Parker and Brian J. Fraser. Toronto: United Church Publishing House, 1989.

Shriver, Donald W. Jr. *Honest Patriots: Loving a Country Enough to Remember Its Misdeeds*. Oxford: Oxford University Press, 2005.

Smylie, Robert F. "A Presbyterian Witness on War and Peace: An Historical Interpretation." *Journal of Presbyterian History* 59, no. 4 (Winter, 1981): 498–516.

Stassen, Glen, Rodney L. Petersen, and Timothy Norton, eds. *Formation for Life: Just Peacemaking and Twenty-First Century Discipleship*. Eugene, OR: Pickwick Press, 2013.

Stone, Ronald H., and Dana Wilbanks, eds. *The Peacemaking Struggle: Militarism & Resistance*. Lanham, MD: University Press of America, 1985.

Stone, Ronald H., and Robert L. Stivers, eds. *Resistance and Theological Ethics*. Lanham, MD: Rowman & Littlefield, 2004.

Wolterstorff, Nicholas. *Until Justice & Peace Embrace*. Grand Rapids: Wm. B. Eerdmans Publishing Co., 1983.

Young, Kathy, ed. *The Promise of Peace*. Church & Society (September/October 1983): 4.

CPSIA information can be obtained
at www.ICGtesting.com
Printed in the USA
FFOW02n0759310717
38212FF